IN YOUR HANDS

A PRACTICAL GUIDE FOR PARENTS IN THE USE OF My BOOK HOUSE PLAN OF CHILD DEVELOPMENT

REVISED EDITION

PUBLISHED BY

THE BOOK HOUSE FOR CHILDREN

CHICAGO

Seventh Printing, 1949

Copyright, 1943

By THE BOOK HOUSE FOR CHILDREN

Printed in U.S.A.

IN YOUR HANDS

Table of Contents

Table of Contents

Table of Contents

Table of Contents

FOREWORD

"In Your Hands" is presented as a guide for parents in understanding and helping their children.

It is designed to aid My BOOK HOUSE parents in the most intelligent use of the graded stories and handwork contained in the My BOOK HOUSE Plan. The direct correlation between the material and the needs and interests of the growing child is made clear.

The charts and Dr. Martin L. Reymert's "The Ladder of Years" are based on data obtained from observation, tests, and school courses of study. However, the standards set up for the average child at each level are not absolute requirements for any individual child; rather, they indicate the stages of development through which each child may be expected to grow at his own rate of speed.

In this edition certain charts which appeared on page 86 and following pages of the previous editions, relating to infants up to the age of 5 years, have been removed. Readers interested in detailed study of norms of mental growth should consult such authoritative publications as Gesell: "First Five Years of Life," Gesell & Ilg: "Infant and Child in The Culture of Today," etc.

In endeavoring to provide both the guidance information and the actual material to use each day with a child, it is our desire to help My BOOK HOUSE parents have a finer, happier relationship with their children.

The Book House for Children

CHAPTER I

Your Child Is in Your Hands!

MANY parents stand in awe when they first read this challenging statement and fully realize the responsibility it places on them in determining the success and happiness of their child.

It was to help the thousands of parents who were finding it so difficult to secure the material they needed to do their all important job successfully that My BOOK HOUSE Plan was developed. With this Plan as a guide you will feel confident that you are using, in your own home, the simple, practical findings of years of research in the field of child study. It will place at your finger tips a guide for understanding and solving many of the problems in child development. It will provide practical answers to your child's training problems *before* the problems arise. Knowing the *right* thing to do at the *right* time will help eliminate fear, uncertainty and emotional upsets in the child's day. Above all, it will prepare you to meet your training problems with the poise and confidence that are necessary to secure your child's happy cooperation and the results you want.

You will find an everyday use for this Plan in your home, and the understanding you gain from this daily contact with the things that go to make up your child's own little world will help you be more sympathetic and understanding in your relationship with him.

The Well-Balanced Child Is the Happy Child. Above everything else, you want your child to develop into a happy, alert, well-balanced individual. The mental diet you select for your child will determine his thoughts and actions and help mold his personality. The child's mental development depends upon a well-balanced mental diet in much the same manner as his physical development depends upon wholesome and nourishing food. The conversations your child hears, the experiences he has, the stories and rhymes you read to him, are all part of his mental diet and greatly influence his thoughts and actions.

My BOOK HOUSE Plan gives your child a choice mental diet that will encourage the development of the very best qualities within him. It will add to your confidence to know that you are prepared to meet the many phases of his development with intelligence and understanding. No "outside the home" training will ever replace the influence of story time in your own home. Children unconsciously pattern their ideals after the thoughts and actions of the people they admire. Your child will be challenged by the truth, honesty, courage and adventure of the characters in the stories you read to him. It has been said that the child cannot learn to think straight unless he has been exposed to the straight thinking of others. In other words, *the child*, like the adult, *becomes what he experiences.* Here, in My BOOK HOUSE, your child will become familiar with some of the world's finest literature and learn to sense its beauty and appeal. The selections will attract and interest him and offer him patterns for living.

Adolescence Really Begins at Birth. The turmoil in the adolescent is sometimes brought about by parents who are unable to understand the problems their child must face at this time. My BOOK

2

IN YOUR HANDS

HOUSE Plan will keep you in close contact with your child's interests as he matures and develops and make you feel more capable of offering him intelligent and sympathetic guidance. Establish confidence in your child during his early years and you will have *earned* his confidence during adolescence. In your daily contacts, help him feel the security that comes with love and understanding and he will experience little difficulty in facing the emotional problems that come with adolescence.

Five Services in My BOOK HOUSE Plan. My BOOK HOUSE Plan brings you, in a form both usable and practical, the concrete help you need to secure the results you want. The twelve beautifully illustrated volumes of My BOOK HOUSE form the basis of the five services the complete My BOOK HOUSE Plan brings to your home. The understanding and close companionship that will result from the use of this specially qualified material in your home will more than repay you for the few minutes you spend each day unfolding it to your child.

PART I of the Plan is represented by the twelve carefully selected and graded volumes of My BOOK HOUSE, which include 2752 pages of graded selections from over fifty different countries. There are over two thousand illustrations—more than half of which are in full color. The extensive Index, found in Volume XII, will prove invaluable to you in choosing the right material for your child's interests at each stage in his development. Character qualities such as confidence, courage, truthfulness, obedience, perseverance and many others that you will want to encourage in your child, are listed in the Child Development Index. Under each of these character qualities you will find the selections that will help you build these same fine qualities in your own child. The more familiar you become with this Index, the more valuable My BOOK HOUSE will become in helping you in your task of training your child.

I N   Y O U R   H A N D S

PART II is this book—the new IN YOUR HANDS. It covers every phase in your child's development from infancy through adolescence. Your attention is focused on each important phase of your child's mental, emotional and social development and reference is made to helpful material in My BOOK HOUSE. The Table of Contents, beginning on page vii of this book, will enable you to quickly locate the material best suited to your needs. It is suggested that you take the time to examine the Table of Contents *before* you introduce your child to My BOOK HOUSE.

PART III is a Packet of CREATIVE WORK FOR YOUR CHILD'S HANDS. It is so important for your child to have access to creative materials in his home in order that he may work out his own ideas. Pages 145 through 174 of IN YOUR HANDS have been devoted to creative expression in children. It is suggested that you become familiar with this material before planning new activities with clay, crayon, paint, etc., for your child.

PART IV of My BOOK HOUSE Plan comes to you in the form of a monthly publication called *YOUR CHILD'S WORLD.* Each month Dr. Martin L. Reymert, an internationally known child psychologist, writes on some phase of child training that is sure to interest you as a parent. In every issue you will find additional articles by specialists in the field of child training that will keep you abreast of the best guidance available.

PART V brings you a FREE CONSULTATION SERVICE. It is included in My BOOK HOUSE Plan to give you the opportunity of consulting our psychologist, Dr. Martin L. Reymert, on your own individual problems. This service has proved invaluable to thousands of parents seeking a satisfactory solution to their child-training problems. You are invited to write to Dr. Reymert, in care of THE BOOK HOUSE FOR CHILDREN.

Appreciation of Literature Begins Early

CHAPTER II

DURING the first two years of the baby's life, he is kept very busy investigating the many new things he is discovering in the world around him. He learns through his sense of feeling, touch, hearing and sight something about the sounds he hears, the objects he sees, and the activities of the people with whom he comes in daily contact. During these early days, then, is the time to lay the foundation for the appreciation of literature in your baby.

Since the baby's hearing is active from birth, the very sound of mother's voice will carry a message to him long before words become meaningful. If the first voices baby hears are rhythmical and pleasing to his little ears, they will bring him a message of love and security. The mother who begins early to sing lullabies and repeat nursery rhymes to her baby is influencing him far more than she realizes. Let your baby hear the soft, soothing lullabies like *Rock-A-Bye, Baby* and *Sweet and Low*, when he is tired and sleepy. Repeat the more lively and playful rhymes like *Rub-a-Dub-Dub* and *Oh, Here's a Leg for a Stocking*, when you are bathing

5

and dressing him. During his playtime, tell him the brisk and active ones like *Pat-a-Cake, Pat-a-Cake, Baker's Man*, *This Little Pig Went to Market*, or *Pease-Porridge Hot*. All these rhymes are about things familiar to your baby, and so they will naturally appeal to him.

Right from the very beginning your baby is forming the habit of listening to the sound of activity around him. He is also learning to identify some of the voices he hears every day. Psychologists tell us that we must first *learn to listen* before we are ready to *listen to learn*. The mother who sings and plays rhymes with her baby encourages him to listen and pay attention right from the beginning of his training.

Introducing Your Baby to My BOOK HOUSE. It is suggested that you try propping your baby up on the davenport or holding him on your lap while you read to him from his book. It is only natural that he will want to examine the colorful pictures on the open page before him. Be sure to give him the opportunity to satisfy his curiosity before you begin reading to him. Placing your finger under the picture that tells about the rhyme you are reading, may help hold his attention. It will also help him to connect the sound and meaning of the words he *hears* with the picture he *sees*. He will, no doubt, show his delight in this new experience by bouncing his arms and legs in time to the rhythm of the rhyme.

A little planning on your part will give your baby a pleasant introduction to his books and literature. When you begin reading, he will listen for only a few brief moments. His attention span is short and so he tires easily. If you notice that he is becoming restless, it is wise to stop, close the book carefully, and carry the baby with you as you return the book to the shelf. The very next day, preferably at the same time, bring his book from the shelf and begin to read to him in much the same manner as you did the day before. Following this very simple procedure with regularity, a few minutes each day, will help your baby form the habit of listening. The period following your baby's bath is usually a very good time for reading.

It will not be long before baby will look forward to his story period with you. You will be pleased to find that he is actually learning to listen and look attentively as you read to him from his book. Gradually, he will want to look and listen for a longer period of time and, by the end of his first year, you will have helped him form the important habit of listening and concentrating that will prove so very valuable to him. You will also find your training problems becoming easier when your baby has mastered this basic habit that will influence all his future learning.

Baby Reflects Your Attitude Toward Books. Children quickly sense your attitude and actions toward books as well as other things. You will find your child imitating the very things you do when handling his book. If, for instance, when you want to turn the page, you will take the time to carefully lift the upper right hand corner of it, and say slowly and rhythmically, *O-V-E-R*, your baby will come to associate the word *over* with the right way to turn pages. As a special treat, let him try to turn a page in his own book and never fail to praise him when he has done it well. He will learn many desirable habits of thoughtfulness and care from seeing you follow this simple procedure each day, and, unconsciously, he will come to look upon his books as objects to be handled with love and care. Make a point of seeing that both your hands and baby's hands are clean before you handle his books and he will want to do likewise. By the time your child is ready to enter first grade, he will have *formed* the habit of handling his books with care, and will be ready to concentrate on the techniques of learning to read. You will have helped him discover the

IN YOUR HANDS

joy of reading and so he will be eager to learn to read for himself in order that he may enjoy the stories he has heard over and over again.

In the first two volumes of My BOOK HOUSE Plan, you will find beautifully illustrated lullabies and rhymes gathered from thirty-three countries of the world, as well as Mother Goose, poems and simple activity and repetitive stories that will interest your baby. By using the Index found in Volume XII of My BOOK HOUSE, you will become more familiar with the fine heritage of children's literature that you want your child to understand and enjoy. The child's taste for literature, later on, will be influenced by the selections you read to him in his preschool and early school years. He will find satisfaction in the sound of good literature and early develop the ability to discriminate between well written stories and trash. The parent who is familiar with the fine background of literature available to children today, is much better equipped to kindle and nurture the appreciation of literature in his own child.

See Language Development and Literature Activities on various charts—pages 80 to 105 of this book.

Language Development Begins at Birth

CHAPTER III

YOUR child's ability to use and understand language will play a most important role in his mental growth and be a valuable asset in helping him adjust himself to new situations and people.

The baby's vocabulary truly begins the moment he hears a word spoken. Mother talks and sings to him for months with no expectation that he will immediately use the language he hears. By the process of constant repetition he begins to understand words, and, later, he attempts to reproduce them. The child, therefore, has a listening, understanding and speaking vocabulary long before he learns to read, write and spell words.

Angelo Patri says, "Children gain their first hint of language and all that belongs to it, by listening. If the first tones he hears are clear, clean-cut and musical, his language will follow the pattern closely."

Speech Habits Formed Early. Since children learn to use language by listening, the wise parent will take every precaution to see that the baby forms good habits of speech. If you expose your baby to good speech from the very beginning, he will come to accept it as his own and pattern his language after the words and sounds he hears. Baby talk and talking down to the child, instead of talking

9

with him, may hamper his desire and ability to use language. The child develops language ability very rapidly during his preschool years and the style of his speech will definitely reflect the influence of his early home environment. In fact, educators agree that the conditions which most affect the child's language development have taken place in his own home, long before he enters school.

Give Him Opportunities to Use Language. You will find almost every part of speech represented in *the two-year-old's* vocabulary. If he has the ability to convey his needs, thoughts and desires in language, he will have less reason to indulge in tantrums and emotional upsets. The child who is unable to express himself in language frequently develops unsocial tendencies as an outlet for his pent-up emotions. The little child has need of language in his everyday living, and if he learns early to talk things over sensibly, he will have achieved something that will be very valuable to him throughout his entire life. Language has proved invaluable to the little child in emergencies, and has often saved the parent needless anxiety. If, when shopping with mother, the child has had experience giving his name and address to the clerk at the store, he will not hesitate to give it to the policeman—should he ever get lost. And, what a help it is in time of illness if the little child is able to tell you about his aches and pains!

Language development is sometimes delayed in the child by anxious parents who anticipate his every need and thus

LANGUAGE DEVELOPMENT

deprive him of opportunities to express himself. Language may be encouraged by framing questions in such a manner that they require an answer in words. For example: When your child is looking at a picture of a horse, if you were to ask him, "Where is the horse?" he could answer this question by *touching* the picture. If, on the other hand, you were to ask, "What is it?" he would need to use *words* . . . "Horse," or "A horse," . . . to answer your question.

Give your child opportunities to use the language he is hearing every day. Let him be a special messenger who delivers simple messages to other members of the family. Be sure to keep these first messages brief so that he will have confidence in his own ability to repeat them correctly. Send him on errands to the store where it is necessary for him to ask the clerk for *one* or *two* items.

Be careful to give the child an audience when he attempts to tell you something, and be generous in your praise when he has expressed himself well. Conversation flows freely over the dinner table, and you will want your child to be able to share in the conversation without dominating the situation.

Stories and Experiences Stimulate Language. Stories and firsthand experiences will give the child interesting things to talk about and help develop his ability to express himself. Dramatization of simple stories, puppet and shadow plays, homemade movies, and creative handwork, are excellent mediums to stimulate the development of language in your child.[1]

My BOOK HOUSE plans for your child's language development long before he learns to talk. Begin by saying and singing some of these choice lullabies and rhymes to him and you will be

[1]See Clay Modeling, page 149; Give Your Child Crayon and Paint, page 166; Happy Hours with Scissors, Cutting, Folding and Pasting, page 161; Dramatic Play, page 177 of IN YOUR HANDS and Packet of *Creative Work for Your Child's Hands.*

IN YOUR HANDS

providing the words, phrases and sentences that will form his own listening vocabulary. The child's ability to use and understand language later on, will be influenced by the listening vocabulary you have exposed him to in babyhood.

Language Development Varies in Children. Language development will vary in the individual child according to his physical and mental maturity. The charts following will help indicate the general vocabulary growth of children during the first five years. These charts have been prepared for My BOOK HOUSE by Martin L. Reymert, Ph.D., Director of the Mooseheart Laboratory for Child Research.

AVERAGE VOCABULARIES OF CHILDREN
Up to 5 years, 6 months of age

Age yr.	mo.	New Words	Total Number of Words
	10	0	0
1	0	3	3
1	6	14	17
2	0	255	272
2	6	134	406
3	0	490	896
3	6	354	1250
4	0	290	1540
4	6	179	1719
5	0	353	2072
5	6	1472	3544

The above table is based on the average of several hundred children. It is interesting to compare these results which were obtained with *actual groups of children* of various ages with the *expected* size of vocabularies indicated in the growth curve on the opposite page. There are variations. Just as actual groups of children will be found to vary from the standard, so an individual child will probably be found to vary with more or less words than the number given for that age. Insofar as vocabulary is a product of the home environment, the development of a good vocabulary, both in size and kind of words, can be materially aided with the selected readings of My BOOK HOUSE.

LANGUAGE DEVELOPMENT

A GENERAL GROWTH CURVE ON THE DEVELOPMENT OF

LANGUAGE ABILITY

6th YEAR

5 yr.   He is most interested in meaning of single words.
5 yr.   He has lost baby talk and knows 2000 words.

END OF
5th YEAR

4 yr.   He can make puns; he converses logically.
4 yr.   His speech implies abstract and rational thinking.

END OF
4th YEAR

3 yr.   He likes to act as he talks. His vocabulary is 1000 words.
3 yr.   His sentences are more expressive of his thoughts.

END OF
3rd YEAR

2 yr.   He now likes to listen to stories about familiar things.
2 yr.   He makes sentences of 1, 2 or 3 words in a sing-song style.
2 yr.   He knows 300 words, but has only a few at his command.

END OF
2nd YEAR

18 mo.   He will say "thank you," instead of "ta ta."
18 mo.   He converses in jargon, but begins to drop baby talk.
18 mo.   He has a vocabulary of 10 words; combines gestures with words.
1 yr.   He obeys simple commands. He can imitate and repeat words.

END OF
1st YEAR

40 wks.   He can recognize his name, and understands "no, no."
40 wks.   He begins to show control of muscles of speech.
28 wks.   He crows and squeals. He is able to judge tones of voice.
16 wks.   He bubbles, coos, chuckles, gurgles and laughs. He heeds voices.
4 wks.   The infant mews and makes guttural sounds. He listens to sound.

BIRTH

13

IN YOUR HANDS

Vocabulary Aids Readiness. It is generally agreed that if the child were solely dependent on the vocabulary he hears at home, he would be at a loss to learn the larger number of new words he is expected to use and understand in the schoolroom. Stories and rhymes that have been carefully graded and illustrated will help give your child a choice variety of words that he will begin to use as his own.

My BOOK HOUSE has been planned to give your child the opportunity of hearing a good descriptive vocabulary used over and over again—a vocabulary that will make his speech more interesting and colorful. In the first three volumes alone, he will hear 6800 different words used in a variety of interesting stories that he will understand and enjoy. By the time he is ready to enter first grade, your child will have become familiar with words and phrases that will give him confidence to express himself freely. The child with a good vocabulary is equipped to understand the language of the teacher, follow directions, and exchange ideas. *He will be ready to learn!* An enriched vocabulary will make him familiar with the sound and meaning of words and be a real help to him as he learns to read.

Influence of Environment. Van Alstyne[2] made an investigation of environmental factors influencing the vocabulary of three-year-old children. She lists the following fifteen factors:

1. Suitable play materials and books.
2. Conversation with child by adults.
3. Proper physical surroundings and routine.
4. Other children in the home.
5. Association with other children.
6. Good economic conditions.
7. Suitable excursions.

[2]Reprinted from D. Van Alstyne, *The Environment of Three-Year-Old Children*, 1929, p. 6, by permission of Teachers College, Columbia University, Bureau of Publications.

LANGUAGE DEVELOPMENT

8. Social atmosphere in the home, visits to others, etc.
9. Responsibility for certain personal and household tasks.
10. Reading to the child.
11. Parent's use of good English.
12. Educational status of parents.
13. Stimulation of independent activity.
14. Interest of parents in the child's activity.
15. Knowledge of level reached by the child and interest in his reaching the next state.

Pictures Give Clue to Meaning of Words. The illustrations in My BOOK HOUSE play an important part in adding meaning to the words your child hears when you read rhymes and stories to him. For example: On page 85 in Volume I, you will find the rhyme,

> *All the cats consulted;*
> *What was it about?*
> *How to catch a little mouse*
> *Running in and out.*

The illustration pictures a group of cats that are quite obviously "talking things over." As the child *hears* the word "consulted" in the rhyme, he *observes* the picture, and, thus, he associates the sound of the word "consulted" with the meaning conveyed in the picture. The rhyme and picture together have helped him form a concept of meaning about the new word he has heard. In the last line of *Tom, Tom, the Piper's Son*, on page 34 of Volume I, the child hears, "Even pigs on their hind legs would after him prance." The picture illustrating this rhyme includes two little "prancing" pigs to help the child form a more meaningful concept of the new word "prance."

In the South American rhyme at the top of page 68 in

15

IN YOUR HANDS

Volume I, there is a whimsical little rhyme about two toads.

The toads in the lake
When it rains pitter-pat-
Some ask for a cap
And some ask for a hat.

One part of the Reading Readiness Test,[3] given to children entering first grade, touches on vocabulary. Each child is given a booklet containing pictures of familiar objects. In one instance, the child must follow the direction, "Put a mark on the *cap*."[4]   This may seem a very simple direction to you but the results of the tests have proved that unless this vocabulary difference has been pointed out to the child in his daily experiences, he will invariably put a mark on the *hat* instead of the *cap*. Another example from this test is pictured here. The child is asked to look at this picture of two boats, and told to "Put a mark on the boat with the sail."[4] Here again, he will be at a loss to know which picture to mark unless he has associated the meaning of the word *sailboat* with the sailboat itself.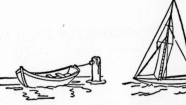

These Reading Readiness Tests are given to discover what the child has learned during his preschool years at home. It is important that children have accurate illustrations in their story books so they will be able to associate the new words they *hear* with the things they *see*.

[3]Pictures from Reading Readiness Tests for Entering First Grade Pupils, based on the Alice and Jerry books, used by permission of the copyright owners, Row, Peterson and Company, Evanston, Illinois.
[4]See reference list, page 19.

LANGUAGE DEVELOPMENT

Good Literature Influences Speech. Rhymes, poems and stories are a natural source for descriptive words that we fail to include in our conversation with little children. At the bottom of page 90 in Volume I, you will find the rhyme,

> *Bye-O! Bye-O!*
> *Baby's in the cradle sleeping.*
> *Tip-toe, tip-toe,*
> *Soft and low, like pussy creeping,*
> *Bye-O, Bye-O!*

The child who hears this rhyme repeated will be exposed naturally to the beauty and charm of language found in the phrase, "Soft and low, like pussy creeping."

Rhymes and stories play an important part in the child's language development. The child will unconsciously pattern his language after the language in the stories you read to him. Little children use the words, phrases and sentences in their favorite stories to relate their own experiences. It is so important that the stories your child hears are well written in short, well-knit sentences.

In Volume I, on page 165, in the story, *Good Morning, Peter*, the child hears sentences like these— " . . . . 'Hello, Teddy Bear!' That is what Peter said. But Teddy Bear said nothing . . . . " This story is typical of the many familiar everyday experiences that are told in a very logical and direct manner.

In Volume I, on pages 190 and 200, you will find stories about the rain and wind told in language simple enough for the child to use as his own. In *A Story of the Wind* (Volume I, page 200) the child hears interesting sentences like, " . . . . The dry leaves in the grass began to hop and flutter and fly around over the ground . . . . The trees all started to shiver, to shiver and shiver and shake . . . . The wind went capering around until it came

17

bolting down . . . . They danced and skipped and jumped and tugged . . . . '' The manner in which your child relates his own experiences will be as free, spontaneous and interesting as the words in the stories you read to him.

Frequently children experience difficulty in relating a series of events or sticking to the subject they are talking about. The child who hears good literature will have the advantage of hearing a story told in logical order, and his own thinking and speech is certain to be influenced by the organization of the stories he has heard.

Language Develops Personality. It is important for you, the parent, to understand your child's language development in order that you can best encourage its growth. Every phase of this development has been planned and pro-vided for in My BOOK HOUSE.  The selections have been carefully graded to help give the child the background he needs as he grows and matures. The child's vocabulary will grow along with his experiences and will be greatly influenced by his choice of reading. Class discussions, assembly programs, club activities, hobbies, and class offices, will be all the more attractive and interesting to the child who can express himself well. The high school student who has a good vocabulary will possess confidence, poise, and the assurance he needs to initiate his ideas and assume the role of leadership.

You have often heard it said that "Speech is golden." Encourage language ability and a good vocabulary and you will open

LANGUAGE DEVELOPMENT

avenues that will promote happiness, understanding, and an interesting personality in your child.

References. Typical references indicating vocabulary differences which are pointed out to the child in My BOOK HOUSE selections:

Boats

I Saw a Ship A-Sailing—Vol. I, page 35
Row, Row, to the Fishing Banks Fare—Vol. I, page 61
Little Beppo Pippo—Vol. I, page 63
Here We Sail So Fast and Free—Vol. I, page 96
My Boat—Vol. I, page 163

Hat and Cap

The Toads in the Lake—Vol. I, page 68
When I See a Lady—Vol. I, page 69
Hurry Up, Engine—Vol. I, page 92
Yankee Doodle—Vol. I, page 101
The Cap That Mother Made—Vol. III, page 12

See Language and Literature Activities on various charts on pages 80 to 105 of IN YOUR HANDS and selections listed in Index of My BOOK HOUSE, Volume XII, under Language and Literature.

CHAPTER IV

Finger Plays Do Much More Than Amuse!

DOWN through the ages mothers have delighted in talking and playing with their babies to win their smiles, coos and gurgles. However, few of these mothers have ever stopped to realize the far-reaching influence this play will have in encouraging a happy, cooperative disposition in their babies. The mother who takes the time to talk and play with her little baby is doing much more than amusing him. In reality, she is helping her child form the important habits of listening and concentrating. She is encouraging the qualities of alertness and curiosity in him that are so important in any individual.

Finger plays and action rhymes like *Pat-a-Cake, Pat-a-Cake, Baker's Man* and *This Little Pig Went to Market*, will help satisfy the baby's natural instinct for play and action.

The baby's ability to understand and use language is very closely tied up with his sensory experiences—his experiences with hearing, feeling, touching, seeing, tasting and smelling. The baby uses his senses to become familiar with the things around him. He becomes aware of his ears, nose, eyes, mouth, toes and hair by touching them. He learns about mother's dress and the shape

FINGER PLAYS

and composition of his bottle and rattle from touching them with his little fingers. He learns to recognize the sound of his rattle, the song of birds, the meow of the cat and the bark of the dog, by listening. He quickly learns to distinguish the sound of the voices of the people who care for his needs. From the very beginning he associates security or annoyance with the tone of the voices he hears. The rhythm and sound of words in lullabies, rhymes and jingles appeal to the baby. He uses his sense of smell to help identify his baby powder, olive oil, orange juice, and so forth. And it is a well known fact that his sense of taste serves to satisfy his curiosity when all other senses have failed him. Although the baby gets many other impressions through his sense of sight— as soon as he discovers light and dark and form and color—he depends much less on this sense than the adult.

Sensory experiences are very valuable to the baby and help give him concrete impressions that urge him to express himself in sound and action. He can amuse himself endlessly by examining his toes and fingers. He thoroughly enjoys having mother talk to him and repeat lilting lullabies and jingles that call for action with his own fingers and toes.

Baby authorities agree that the baby must first master certain rhythmical body movements before he is ready to learn to walk and talk. Finger plays and simple games where the baby plays an active part provide opportunities for him to gain control of his own body, and encourage good disposition qualities in him. Baby must pay very close attention to mother if he wants to hear, see and do the things mother is doing as she plays with him. He learns early to detect changes in the sound of her voice and to follow her motions. The following finger plays have been especially prepared to accompany the rhymes in My BOOK HOUSE. These plays will encourage the baby to enter into the activity spontaneously.

21

IN YOUR HANDS

See-Saw Sacaradown
Volume 1, Page 18

See-saw, sacaradown,
*   Which is the way to London town?*
One foot up, the other down,
*   This is the way to London town.*

Pat-a-Cake, Pat-a-Cake, Baker's Man
Volume 1, Page 19

Pat-a-cake, pat-a-cake, baker's man!
*   Make me a cake as fast as you can;*
Prick it, and pat it, and mark it with T,
*   And put it in the oven for Tommy*
and me.

This Little Pig Went to Market
Volume 1, Page 19

This little pig went to market;
*   This little pig stayed at home;*
*   This little pig had roast beef;*
This little pig had none;
*   This little pig said, "Wee, wee, wee!*
*   I can't find my way home!"*

22

See-Saw Sacaradown

Volume 1, Page 18

Mother plays this rhyme with child lying down in his crib, baby carriage or couch. Lift baby's right and left leg, up and down, alternately in "see-saw" motion, as you say the words of the rhyme.

Pat-a-Cake, Pat-a-Cake, Baker's Man
Volume 1, Page 19

At first, mother will hold baby's little wrists in her own hands and clap his hands together rhythmically as she says the rhyme. Later, she may repeat the rhyme, facing the baby so he can see what she is doing, and clap her own hands as she repeats the words. The baby will soon try imitating mother's actions with his own little hands. After mother has played the rhyme with baby a few times, he will begin to clap his own hands together when he hears the words of the rhyme.

For suggestion for older child, see page 30.

This Little Pig Went to Market
Volume 1, Page 19

Mother will play this with her baby by touching each toe as she tells about the five little pigs in the rhyme. When she comes to the last little pig who cried, "Wee, wee, wee," she can wiggle the baby's little toe. Mother can also play this rhyme with her baby using his fingers instead of his toes.

Hickory, Dickory, Dock
Volume 1, Page 22

Hickory, dickory, dock!
The mouse ran up the clock;
The clock struck one, the mouse ran
*   down,*
Hickory, dickory, dock!

Jack and Jill Went up the Hill
Volume 1, Page 40

Jack and Jill went up the hill
*   To fetch a pail of water;*
Jack fell down and broke his crown
And Jill came tumbling after.

Humpty Dumpty Sat on a Wall
Volume 1, Page 46

Humpty Dumpty sat on a wall,
Humpty Dumpty had a great fall.
All the king's horses, and all the king's
*   men,*
Couldn't put Humpty Dumpty together
*   again.*

24

FINGER PLAYS

Hickory, Dickory, Dock
Volume 1, Page 22

Nod head from side to side to the words "Hickory, dickory, dock." Raise both arms as high as you can reach, with fingers in motion, as you say the line, "The mouse ran up the clock." Keep arms raised over head and clap hands together for the line, "The clock struck one." Return arms to side with fingers in motion to the line, "The mouse ran down." Finish with nods of head from right to left to the last line, "Hickory, dickory, dock."

Jack and Jill Went up the Hill
Volume 1, Page 40

Raise both arms over your head as you repeat the line, "Jack and Jill went up the hill, etc." Drop one arm suddenly to the line, "Jack fell down and broke his crown." Drop the other arm suddenly to the line, "And Jill came tumbling after."

Humpty Dumpty Sat on a Wall
Volume 1, Page 46

Hold hands together in clapping position as you say, "Humpty Dumpty sat on a wall." Drop hands to lap suddenly to the line, "Humpty Dumpty had a great fall." Turn hands palms up and spread fingers apart to line, "All the king's horses and all the king's men, etc."

Pease-Porridge Hot, Pease-Porridge Cold
Volume 1, Page 47

Pease-porridge hot, pease-porridge cold,
Pease-porridge in the pot, nine days
old.
Some like it hot, some like it cold,
Some like it in the pot, nine days old.

There Were Two Blackbirds
Volume 1, Page 51

There were two blackbirds
Sitting on a hill,
The one named Jack,
And the other named Jill.
Fly away, Jack!
Fly away, Jill!
Come again, Jack!
Come again, Jill!

Row, Row, to the Fishing Banks Fare
Volume 1, Page 61

Row, row, to the fishing banks fare!
How many fishes did you catch there?
One for father, one for mother,
One for sister, one for brother,
And one for the little fisher boy.

26

Pease-Porridge Hot, Pease-Porridge Cold
Volume 1, Page 47

For tiny baby clap hands together three times to words, "Pease-porridge hot." Repeat for "Pease-porridge cold." Clap hands gently against baby's legs to line, "Pease-porridge in the pot, nine days old." Repeat action of first line for the third line. Repeat action of the second line for the fourth line.

There Were Two Blackbirds
Volume 1, Page 51

"There were two blackbirds"—*with this line make fists with thumbs extended.*
"Sitting on a hill,"—*bring fists together.*
"The one named Jack,"—*extend right fist.*
"And the other named Jill."—*extend left fist.*
"Fly away, Jack!"—*open right hand and move hand outward in fluttering motion.*
"Fly away, Jill!"—*open left hand, etc.*
"Come again, Jack! Come again, Jill!"—*with these lines bring hands back to starting position.*

Row, Row, to the Fishing Banks Fare
Volume 1, Page 61

"Row, row, to the fishing banks fare!"—with this line move arms back and forth in rowing motion. Continue same movement with line, "How many fishes did you catch there?" Hold left hand in folded position and with right hand unfold each finger beginning with thumb to the line, "One for father, one for mother, etc."

27

Guiseppi, the Cobbler
Volume 1, Page 63

Guiseppi, the cobbler, makes my shoes;
He pounds them, *rap, rap, rap!*
He makes them small, he makes them
   big,
And ever he pounds, *tap, tap!*

Here's the Church
Volume 1, Page 83

Here's the church
And here's the steeple;
Open the door
And see all the people!

John Brown Had a Little Indian
Volume 1, Page 100

John Brown had a little Indian,
One little Indian boy.
One little, two little, three little Indians,
Four little, five little, six little Indians,
Seven little, eight little, nine little
   Indians,
Ten little Indian boys!

28

FINGER PLAYS

Guiseppi, the Cobbler
Volume 1, Page 63

"Guiseppi, the cobbler, makes my shoes; he pounds them, rap, rap, rap!"—with these lines tap fists together in time with the rhyme. Hold hands close together as you say, "He makes them small." Spread hands further apart to the line, "He makes them big." Tap fists together again to line, "And ever he pounds, tap, tap!"

Here's the Church
Volume 1, Page 83

(*For younger child*)
With line, "Here's the church," interlock fingers.
"And here's the steeple"—extend forefingers.
"Open the door"—spread thumbs apart.
Unfold fingers and wiggle them to line, "and see all the people!"
(*Traditional for older child*)
Children lock hands, fingers down, thumbs close together to represent the church door, and forefingers up and joined for the spire. With "Open the door!" they open their hands, fingers still locked, and wiggle the fingers to represent the people.

John Brown Had a Little Indian
Volume 1, Page 100

(*For the baby*)
Fold baby's hands in fists. With the line, "John Brown had a little Indian," unfold the thumb of baby's right hand and continue unfolding each finger on each hand until all ten fingers are unfolded. The child from two years on, will want to make his own fingers do just what the rhyme says.

IN YOUR HANDS

Finger plays help develop alertness in the young baby and he soon comes to associate certain actions with the sound of words and phrases he hears mother repeat in rhymes and jingles. The baby forms habits of speech very early and so it is important that the language your baby hears from the very beginning is rhythmical, clean-cut and musical. The love of good language will color your baby's impressions and his own speech will reflect the same language qualities he has heard from birth.

Additional action rhymes and jingles to play with your baby are listed in the Index of My BOOK HOUSE, Volume XII, on page 291 under *Play*.

Pat-a-Cake, Pat-a-Cake, Baker's Man!

Volume 1, Page 19

(Suggestion for older child)

The older child will enjoy a little variety in the actions for "Pat-a-cake, etc." Here is a suggested form. Clap hands in rhythm with the first line of the rhyme. Then for the line, "Prick it, and pat it"—fold right hand in a fist and extend forefinger. Now, make a motion similar to one you would use if you were to prick the top of a pie, and then *pat* your hands together. For the remainder of the line, "and mark it with T"—hold the left hand straight up and rigid and place the right hand across the top of it to form the letter "T". For the last line, "And put it in the oven for Tommy and me," extend both hands forward—palms up—as if you were actually putting a pan of cookies in the oven. Using the right hand, point away from you to indicate Tommy and toward you to indicate yourself.

CHAPTER V

Bring Out the Best in Your Child's Personality

YOUR child's happiness will depend on his ability to get along well with others. The habits he forms, his character and personality development, will largely determine his poise and success in life. Most parents find the task of guiding and encouraging the growth of fine character qualities and disposition traits a never-ending job. There is no magic that will immediately instill them in the child and, yet, since we know his success and happiness will depend on them, we must constantly nurture them. The attitudes you build in your child from day to day will play an important role in deciding his conduct and actions as well as his ability to get along with others.

The baby begins his formation of habits and disposition traits from birth. As early as twenty-four hours old he may exhibit signs of temper, annoyance or contentment. The first habits baby forms are emotional and mental as well as physical, and so the parent must be concerned with his emotional reactions and disposition traits from the very beginning.

Little children are sensitive and quick to imitate the attitudes as well as the actions of the people around them. The infant unconsciously reflects mother's attitude of cheerfulness or annoyance. Likewise, he gathers his understanding of truth, kindness and

31

helpfulness from the actions of people in his own home. It does not take him long to discover what pleases or annoys and to use the policy which brings him immediate results.

Parents Decide Atmosphere of the Home. The first duty of parents, then, should be to take an inventory of their *own* emotional reactions to see that baby is exposed to desirable disposition qualities in the home. The urge to be cheerful, thoughtful and friendly is *caught* rather than *taught.* The child quickly accepts cheerfulness, good nature, love, friendliness, courage or sullenness as the order of the day, and it is only natural that the attitudes he is exposed to most frequently will become more or less automatic with him. Parents quite unconsciously decide the atmosphere in their home by their daily mode of living. The child whose parents scurry through breakfast and rush off to work is most likely the child who starts his school day in the same flustered manner. Emotional and social habits are largely the result of family relationships and so the parent is responsible for setting the stage for good habit formation and dispositions. Love and understanding, firmness and justice, will encourage the development of the best qualities in your child. Kindness and helpfulness in the home will help bring out courtesy and friendliness in your child's nature. The tone of your voice, your mannerisms, the touch of your hands when you bathe and dress him, give your baby a clue to your frame of mind and challenge him to match your attitude and disposition.

Do not expect perfection in your child's behavior and be careful that you are not demanding more of him than he is capable of giving. The growth of worthwhile habits, character qualities and an attractive personality is a gradual one and cannot be hurried. Temper tantrums and *no, I won'ts* frequently result from exposing the child to situations he is unable to cope with successfully. They reveal his feeling of frustration and indicate his lack

32

of confidence to meet the situation at hand. Emotions are among the most powerful influences in life and the little child, as well as the adult, gains the necessary poise and ability to guide and control them through experience, perseverance and desire.

Importance of Habit Formation. The habits the little child forms soon become automatic and help ease the strain of the day's routine. As soon as he has formed habits that help him in eating, dressing, putting his toys away, etc., he will be relieved of emotional strain and find more joy in his activities. By the time he is *five*, the child should possess a set of habits that will leave him free to initiate ideas, think things through for himself, concentrate, and act independently. Kindergarten and first grade programs are planned around children who are ready to act and think independently. The habits your child forms during his early years, his character and personality development, will largely determine his readiness for learning and his ability to make adjustments with his friends and playmates.

Stories Influence Character Development. Accept your child's offer to help and encourage his independence at every stage where he is capable of assuming responsibility for his own actions. Give him plenty of time to try his hand at putting his toys away, buttoning and unbuttoning his clothes, and attempting to feed himself with his unskilled hands. Hurrying him in this initial stage of independence will only confuse and rob him of the thrill that comes with accomplishment. It is important that he be cooperative when he is getting washed and dressed, that he go to bed willingly, and be cheerful and friendly in his contacts with people. The little child instinctively imitates what he sees and hears, and rhymes and stories that present friendliness, willing obedience, truthfulness and self-control in an attractive manner, will suggest many desirable qualities that he will accept as his own. A variety of rhymes and stories that will help bring out these qualities in your child are listed in the Index, Volume XII, under Child's Daily Activities on page 283. The Finger Plays beginning on page 20 of this book will encourage a happy, cheerful disposition in your baby; while stories similar to *Good Morning, Peter* (Volume I, page 165), will delight and challenge the youngster who is learning to dress himself. Do not attempt to moralize the stories you read to him. Let them tell their own message in the delightful story language that your child understands and enjoys.

In the Index, Volume XII, you will find graded selections listed under character qualities such as Courage, Honesty, Leadership, Obedience, Perseverance and Self-Control. For example, the story of *The Little Engine That Could* (Volume II, page 200), is listed under Perseverance. Every child will enjoy hearing about the plucky Little Engine that worked so hard to pull the trainload of toys over a high mountain so the children who lived on the other side could have them in time for Christmas. The Engine kept saying, "I think I can! I think I can!" The mountain side was steep and the load was heavy but the Little Engine kept trying and saying, "I think I can!" until it finished what it had started out to do. It then ran gaily down the other side of the mountain saying, "I thought I could! I thought I could!"

Perhaps you will find your child imitating the Little Engine with this "I think I can! I thought I could!" attitude when he is putting his toys away or doing some other chore around the house. This will sound so much more pleasant than, "I can't do it, Mother." And this "I think I can!" attitude will serve him well in so many situations throughout life.

Stories present life situations to the child in a personal way and act as an incentive for him to develop the same tolerance, loyalty and courage manifested in his story friends. They are an important part of his mental diet and a vital influence in help-

YOUR CHILD'S PERSONALITY

ing him form his own code for living. By carefully choosing your story from the Index in Volume XII, you will often be touching on little situations that have come up in your child's day. The solution the story character finds for his problem may well be the one that will help smooth over a situation that has been hampering a pleasant and intimate relationship in the home or at school. Make use of a story background and you will find yourself looking at your child's behavior more objectively and impersonally.

Encourage Your Child to Make Decisions. It is often easier for parents to give a command than it is for them to use the ingenuity that is required for intelligent control of a behavior situation. The child who is taught only through discipline is very often helpless in a real-life situation. You want your child to feel adequate to make simple decisions for himself when he is in school or at play. You want to fortify him to act with confidence and to feel capable of deciding things for himself. If you continually teach him to wait for your decision before he acts, he will lose many opportunities to think for himself. The manner in which he is able to meet his everyday problems *now* will help him make decisions in more complex problems later on. Right now, he may be called upon to decide such problems as whether or not to cross the street to Bobby's house; to admit or deny his part in the breaking of a toy or window; or to visit friends without first telling mother of his plans. Your child's ability to make his own decisions in these situations will depend largely on his background of firsthand and story experiences.

My BOOK HOUSE is filled with characters from the literature of the world who will influence your child's personality and make him more tolerant and considerate of the opinions and customs of others. Stories help enrich the child's experiences and give him the benefit of hearing others make wise decisions. He will

35

readily accept the desirable behavior patterns and decisions of the storybook and real friends he admires. Just imagine the impression *The Tale of Peter Rabbit* (Volume II, page 112) would have on the little child who is reluctant to obey mother's requests on matters important to his safety and welfare. It is quite within the child's comprehension to decide that Peter was most foolish to disobey mother's advice, "..... don't go into Mr. McGregor's garden." He is relieved when the little rabbit arrives home safely but, at the same time, he feels quite satisfied that Peter has been justly treated when his mother puts him to bed with only camomile tea for supper. He even feels tempted to tell Peter how unwise he has been! A background of stories will add to your child's ability to make wise decisions, and time and time again you will find him drawing the same conclusion as his story friends.

Reading Background Aids Adjustments. As your child grows, his reading background will influence his thoughts and actions tremendously. He will discover admirable characters in literature that he will want to imitate. For instance, the reading of *A Boy on the High Seas* (Volume VIII, page 8), brings the child in contact with Joshua Barney, the young boy who discovered that physical strength alone does not make a leader. He worked with "..... men far older and more experienced than he, but for all their great hairy chests and the powerful strength of their muscles, they had no ability to lead, to plan, or to command." The child discovers through this story that it is not only desirable to be a leader but that one must know how to follow good leadership intelligently.

Be patient and ready to praise your child's sincere efforts to adjust himself to the situations he must meet. It is only in this manner that he will acquire the poise and self-assurance he needs to adjust himself to situations in life. The child who is able to make adjustments with ease and confidence will feel at home with

YOUR CHILD'S PERSONALITY

people and possess one of the most valuable assets for assuring his continued success and happiness.

CONSULTATION SERVICE

In addition to the actual character building selections in the Index, Volume XII, My BOOK HOUSE Plan offers free consultation service[1] to parents on disposition habits, character qualities and behavior problems.

REFERENCES

A few examples of the character building selections in My BOOK HOUSE are listed below. For complete list, see Index of My BOOK HOUSE, Volume XII, page 284.

Courage

Shingebiss, the brave, cheery, little brown duck, (Volume II, page 96) will help your child overcome fear, timidity and shyness, and encourage him to stick to the task at hand, no matter how discouraging the outlook.

Cooperation

Li'l' Hannibal (Volume III, page 116) was unwilling to do his share so he decided to run away and live with the birds and animals. But no one could stop and play—there was too much work to be done! When Li'l' Hannibal learned that he couldn't have any supper because he hadn't helped, he decided for *himself* that he had better go home and be willing to do his share. Your child will learn from this story to cooperate and to see a thing through to a finish.

Perseverance

The story of little Franz, *The Luck Boy of Toy Valley* (Volume VI, page 108), who had the determination and persistence to keep on trying until his wood carving was com-

[1] See Part IV of the My BOOK HOUSE Plan—page 4 of this book.

37

plete, will help your child if he is inclined toward discouragement or if he is tempted to give up too easily. Every child will love this story of the little boy who started a whole industry by carving a toy sheep out of wood.

Lack of money for paints and the ridicule of the villagers did not keep Titian from clinging to his determination to become a great artist. Through his own initiative he discovered that he could paint with colors from crushed flower petals and, in this way, proved that he was not an impractical dreamer. This story, *The Boy Who Made His Own Materials* (Volume VI, page 114), will help give your child the courage to carry his own ideas through to a finish in order to prove their worth.

Stubbornness

The first indication of stubbornness may not seem serious but if this trait is not corrected it may become a habit. The antics of the "Big, Contrary Coo" in the story *The Wee, Wee Mannie and the Big, Big Coo* (Volume III, page 99), will help your child see how foolish it is to be stubborn. He will decide for himself that he does not want to be like the ridiculous old cow who simply "would not stand still."

See charts in this book:
Social Behavior and Adjustment Qualities for Kindergarten—page 80.
Social Behavior and Adjustment Qualities for Grades One, Two and Three—page 86.
Social Behavior for Grades Four, Five and Six—page 94.
Citizenship for Grades Seven, Eight and Nine—page 102.

For selections to encourage desirable habits, attitudes, character and disposition qualities see Index of My BOOK HOUSE, Volume XII, page 284.

Can You Answer Your Child's Questions?

CHAPTER VI

QUESTIONS! Questions! Questions! Most parents are convinced there is nothing more endless than the questions their children ask. It is a real art to answer the child's questions in a manner satisfying to him. The saying, "Patience is a virtue," was never more applicable.

Questioning is Natural Part of Child's Growth. Curiosity and questioning are a natural part of the child's growth. The baby finds the world around him a continual challenge and he is constantly seeking answers to the things that attract his attention and arouse his curiosity. Your child's questions will reflect his thinking and his attempts to reason. They give him an opportunity to practice language and a variety of things to talk about. Then, too, the child must have an audience to question and his thinking process is stimulated by talking with others. Be patient and calm during this trying period in his development, and before long you will acquire the art of answering his questions in a manner that will prove helpful to both of you.

Stages in Questioning. The child's questions are baffling to parents because they must stop to think how to put the answer into language simple enough for the child to understand. If you are familiar with the various stages of questioning in the young child, you will be more successful in your approach. Some questions require only one-word answers, while others must be dealt with in more detail. But, for the most part, parents err on the side of boring the young child with detailed answers beyond his comprehension. Give him an answer to satisfy his present needs and he will come back later when he needs further information.

39

IN YOUR HANDS

Questions of the Two and Three-Year-Old. The *two to three-year-old* asks questions to hear himself talk. He loves to use his newly acquired language and for the most part knows the answers to the questions he asks. He will be satisfied to have you ask *him* the same question he has asked you. This will give him an opportunity to tell you the answer and, above all, he craves your attention and an occasion to talk. "Where's the book?", "See the cow?", and "Where's Bobby?" are typical questions of this age.

The child who questions is thinking and alert, and so his little mind is active and growing. Your own ability to answer your child's questions will establish confidence in him and bring him back again and again to seek your advice. If you continually show irritation and annoyance when he questions you, he may lose his desire to investigate and reason, and seek less desirable ways of satisfying his curiosity.

Questions of the Four and Five-Year-Old. Questioning is at its peak in the *four-year-old* and it will be less puzzling for you to answer his questions if you realize that they do not reflect a hunger for information but rather an impulse to build up meaning about the things around him. His inquiring mind has little knowledge of the past and future and so your answer must suit his needs at the moment. At this age one question seems to invite another, and the child may not even wait until you have answered one question until he frames another. He loves to talk and get your attention more than he seeks an answer. He asks many *why* and *how* questions and is not always interested in explanations. In fact, his questions represent a soliloquy that gives him an opportunity to use language and formulate relationships in his own mind. He gains better control of language through asking questions and adds clauses and adjectives and adverbs to his vocabulary. "I *was* a good boy, wasn't I?" or "I *was* the best runner, wasn't I?"

YOUR CHILD'S QUESTIONS

are typical questions of the four-year-old. Very often there is no answer to the four-year-old's questions and a story that infers the answer will satisfy him best. The traffic signal or steam shovel at the corner will attract his attention and his questions about them will really be his way of thinking out loud about his new experience. "The Big Street in the Big City" (Volume I, page 170), "The Police Cop Man" (Volume I, page 173) and "Biting Marion" (Volume I, page 174) are stories telling of experiences similar to his own. Choose one of these stories to answer his questions and you will not only satisfy his curiosity at the moment, but you will expose him to additional details that he will want to observe for himself.

The child of four or five who questions you about the wind will be more interested in a story or verse that tells about its usefulness than in a scientific explanation.

> *Blow, wind, blow, and go, mill, go!*[1]
> *That the miller may grind his corn;*
> *That the baker may take it,*
> *And into rolls make it,*
> *And send us some hot in the morn.*

This rhyme will not only give him a satisfying answer but will supply him with information that he can understand and enjoy.

The *five-year-old* will be more direct in his questions and be searching for definite information. By five, he no longer asks questions merely for attention and practice in speaking. He will be more interested in knowing how the steam shovel *works* and what *makes* the light turn from green to red. His questions are less annoying than the four-year-old's because they have more meaning and reason for being asked. He will want an answer in terms of *use*, and is able to understand answers with details. He will be interested in knowing that the steam shovel scoops out

[1]Blow, Wind, Blow, B.H. I:31.

dirt and digs holes for basements in homes and buildings. In fact, he is capable of questioning you on the meaning of a particular word. It is easier to answer the five-year-old's questions because he has accumulated a background of experiences that help him understand the things you refer to in your answers.

Stories and Pictures Help Answer Your Child's Questions. Stories about the Boy Hero of Harlem,[2] Sir Roland,[3] Paul Bunyan,[4] Mozart,[5] Theodore Roosevelt,[6] Shakespeare,[7] Joseph and His Brethren,[8] etc., will prove fascinating reading for the child in the grades and give him a background of knowledge that will add interest to his study of history, geography and social science. The biographies in My BOOK HOUSE bring him in contact with fine characters who have contributed to our civilization, and prepare him for his studies in high school and college. The element of fiction running through these selections will help impress the facts and details on his mind and stimulate him to further research and non-fictional reading.

Books and accurate pictures not only help answer the child's questions but enable him to find the answers for himself. Be honest and sincere in your attitude when answering your child's questions and talk to him in a friendly adult manner. When he asks a question that puzzles you, do not be afraid to tell him, "I do not know, but perhaps we can find the answer in My BOOK HOUSE." Throughout the grades the child's curiosity will spur him on to read and investigate in order to find the information he needs. The selections and pictures in My BOOK HOUSE will help you to answer your child's questions to his satisfaction and keep you informed of his interests. Be patient and understanding in your attitude toward his questions and you will help him think things through for himself and discourage the annoying habit of asking "What?" and "Why?" without rhyme or reason.

[2]The Boy Hero of Harlem—B.H., IV:57.   [5]The Duty That Was Not Paid—B.H., VI:159.
[3]The Knights of the Silver Shield—B.H., VII:173.   [6]The Rough Rider—B.H., IX:72.
[4]The Story of Big Paul Bunyan—B.H., IV:161.   [7]Down by the River Avon—B.H., XII:15.
[8]Joseph and His Brethren—B.H., X:48.

YOUR CHILD'S QUESTIONS

REFERENCES

Suggestions for the Young Child

See selections listed in Index of My BOOK HOUSE, Volume XII, under:

[1]See chapter, Dramatic Play, page 177, and List of Selections in My BOOK HOUSE for Encouraging Imitation and Dramatic Play in Your Child (Suggestions for the Young Child), page 184 of this book.

[2]See chapter, Holidays Begin at Home, page 175 of this book.

[3]See chapter, Let Your Child Discover the Joy of Music, page 187.

[4]See chapter, Expose Your Child to Nature Experiences, page 54 of this book.

IN YOUR HANDS

Suggestions for the Older Child

See selections listed in Index of My BOOK HOUSE, Volume XII, under:

[1]See chapter, Clay Modeling, page 149 of this book. See also Packet of *Creative Work for Your Child's Hands.*

[2]See chapter, Dramatic Play, page 177, and List of Selections in My BOOK HOUSE for Encouraging Imitation and Dramatic Play in Your Child (Suggestions for the Older Child), page 186 of this book. See also Packet of *Creative Work for Your Child's Hands.*

[3]See Index of My BOOK HOUSE, Volume XII, for selections about Christopher Columbus, George Washington, Abraham Lincoln, David Farragut, Robert Fulton, Theodore Roosevelt, Daniel Boone, Buffalo Bill, etc.—names are listed alphabetically.

See the following selections for interesting facts of science:

Steam—Volume V, page 45.

Fireworks ⎱
Steamboat ⎰ Volume V, page 48.

Airplane—Volume V, page 66 and Volume VI, page 164.

Paints—Volume VI, pages 114, 164.

Can You Enter into the Spirit of Play with Your Child?

CHAPTER VII

THE parent who is able to enter into the spirit of play with his child is sure to enjoy a priceless intimacy with his thought-life.

Play is spontaneous in childhood. It is vital to the child's growth and well-being, and a natural outlet for his ideas and emotions. The play that gives your child the most satisfaction will also stimulate his initiative, give him confidence, a sense of responsibility, and encourage him to be resourceful. Play provides many opportunities for the child to develop personality and a friendly cooperative spirit toward others.

Furnish ample shelves and chests for toys and play materials in your home and you will greatly simplify your child's task of putting his own things away. The little child gets definite training in responsibility that is meaningful to him when he has a place to house and care for his own toys and belongings.

"Pick Up" Time. Be sure that your attitude at "pick up" time is a cheerful and helpful one and you will be more successful in getting him to cooperate in putting his toys away. Very often children become so deeply engrossed in their play that they are reluctant to obey when told to stop. Nursery and kindergarten teachers have found that the child accepts a signal telling him to put his playthings away more willingly than he will a hurried command, "Put your toys away!" A tap on a dinner gong, a chord on the piano, or the ring of an alarm clock, may well serve as a

45

signal to tell him to plan to end his playtime. Explain that the first signal he hears will be telling him to, "Get ready now!", while the second signal will mean, "Come to mother!" The time allowed between the two signals will depend largely upon the length of time it will take him to do a good job of putting away the toys and materials he has been using. A five-minute period is usually sufficient for "cleaning up." However, it may be necessary to allow more time if there has been block building or activities where there is an unusual amount of materials to be put away.

The little toddler finds real joy and satisfaction in doing things for himself. Early in his training you can help him form the habit of putting his toys away. You will want him to feel that he is doing his part of the job, and some simple statement like, "You put your blocks on the shelf while I put your dog in the cupboard," will help give him a feeling of satisfaction in cooperating. Give some thought to his first play experiences and

you are certain to encourage a more cooperative and helpful attitude in your child. "Pick up" time should serve a definite purpose in training your child in the formation of good work habits.

THE SPIRIT OF PLAY

Choose Toys With Care. Toys and play materials that are wisely chosen will serve many purposes in the child's day. Do not overlook the value of toys made from odds and ends of materials found around the house as they are often more acceptable to the child than the more elaborate and expensive ones you buy at the store.

Psychologists suggest keeping the following in mind when choosing toys for your child:

1. Is it suitable for the child's age?
2. Will it invite activity on his own age level?
   (If it is too simple, it will not appeal to him—if it is too difficult, he will be discouraged by his inability to use it.)
3. Is it practical and suitable for use in your home or yard?
4. Is it sturdy enough for your child to use, and yet attractive in color and design?
5. Is it safe and sanitary?
6. Will it promote and suggest activity that will develop his imagination and satisfy his desire to experiment and explore?

Play Reflects Child's Maturity. The toys children enjoy at different age levels will vary in accordance with their mental maturity and physical development. The child works out his own ideas in his play and so, as his ideas and fund of information grow, the character of his play changes to fit his mental and physical maturity. A background of stories and experiences will help give your child a better knowledge of life around him, develop his imagination and thinking, and give him ideas that he will use in his play experiences.

Suggested helps for introducing your child to play materials and equipment

I T IS important for the parent to give thought to the selection of play equipment and materials. The nature of your child's play will depend largely upon his ability to imagine, recall and reconstruct experiences in his own everyday life. Stories, rhymes, and pictures will prove an invaluable source for feeding and clarifying his ideas. The child's ideas and play activities will go hand in hand as he matures. It is almost impossible for the child to gain all the information and knowledge he needs during his early years, from firsthand experiences. A well-balanced variety of stories on his own level of understanding will help develop and stimulate creativity in the child.

Play Develops Character and Personality. Many of the lasting and basic qualities of character and personality are crystallized in the child during his play contacts. You will want to encourage the following desirable qualities in your child:

Cheerfulness	Justice	Self-control
Cooperation	Leadership	Thoughtfulness
Courage	Originality	Tolerance
Courtesy	Perseverance	Truthfulness
Friendliness	Responsibility	Willingness
Helpfulness	Self-confidence	

THE SPIRIT OF PLAY

The development of these qualities strengthens your child's character and personality and makes him a more desirable member of society. In the Index—Volume XII, pages 284 to 289—you will find stories listed alphabetically under these same character and personality qualities. By carefully choosing your stories from this Index, you will be using the material you need to encourage these qualities in your child.

A FEW RULES FOR THE WORK SHOP

A few simple safety rules for the use of new play equipment will help prevent accidents and enable your child to get the most out of his experiences.

> It is best to supervise the young child when he first begins to use a hammer, nails and saw. All sawing and nailing should be done at the workbench.
> If two children are working together, it is well to keep them far enough apart to prevent bumping.
> Show the beginner the correct way to use new tools and equipment.

Encourage your child to choose materials wisely for size, etc., to prevent waste. Scraps of wood and materials should be saved and stored in a box. Only the tools needed to do the job should be brought out. Discourage unnecessary noise while working. There is a vast difference between the noise of activity and industry and the thoughtless shouts of careless workers.

See Unit No. 10 of *Creative Work for Your Child's Hands.*

IN YOUR HANDS

PLAY ACTIVITIES ENJOYED BY CHILDREN FROM KINDERGARTEN THROUGH THIRD GRADE

Play Houses. Building and equipping play houses with homemade furniture, clay dishes, rugs, etc.

Farm. Building farm houses and barns with blocks, boxes, etc. Making silo, windmill, animal stalls and animals.

Circus. Making circus tents and ticket office, tickets, booths, novelties to sell, toy money, costumes, animals and animal cages.

Post Office. Making mailman's cap and bag. Building post office and making mail boxes. Using stamps for letters and using toy wagons as delivery trucks, etc.

Grocery Store. Building grocery store. Making toy money, clay fruits and vegetables. Using empty cans and cartons for food products, scales and other measures and weights, paper bags, delivery truck, telephone to take orders, and order books to list groceries. Printing of price tags, display stands, etc.

Airports. Building airports and hangars. Using toy airplanes for dramatic play. Making model airplanes, plane instruments, goggles and aviator's cap. Making a plane large enough to sit in out of blocks, barrel, etc.

Fire Station. Building fire stations, engines, from blocks—using toy wagon for a fire engine that will go. Making fire hats, hose and axes and other equipment that will make their play more realistic.

Trains and Depots. Building train, freight cars, ticket office, and depots of blocks, boxes, etc. (A barrel or empty oil keg makes a good engine.) Making tickets.

Help your child to be cooperative and friendly in his first play contacts

CHAPTER VIII

PARENTS can do a great deal to set the stage for friendly play contacts in the home if they are familiar with the social behavior to be expected of the child from babyhood through his preschool years.

Up until the age of *fifteen* or *eighteen months*, the baby will amuse himself for hours in his play pen, walking from one side to the other—stopping again and again to pick up, throw away or examine the toys within his reach. He enjoys lifting objects in and out of a box, basket or pan. His attention span is brief and so he shifts rapidly from one activity to another. He imitates things he sees other members of his family doing, and is perfectly content to be an onlooker to the play of older children.

Generally, by the time the baby is *two*, he is ready to make his first play contacts with other children. While the two-year-old enjoys being in the room with other children, he is frequently at a loss to know how to play with them cooperatively. He knows little of the social give-and-take necessary to group play and is more concerned with investigating the physical make-up of his

51

playmate by grabbing and snatching at his hair or clothing. The child of two rarely asks for help and so it is important for the adult to be ever watchful and ready to give help when he sees it is needed. At the age of two, the power of imitation is strong in the child and he will invariably want to play with the same toy his playmate is using. Psychologists frequently refer to the two-year-old's interest in "parallel play." For example: If Bobby is playing with a cuddly toy bunny, you may be sure that no other toy will satisfy your child. It is a good idea, then, for the mother of a two-year-old, to plan for the visit of a playmate in order to prevent unnecessary squabbling and tears. Put most of your child's toys out of sight for these occasions, and leave out only one or two duplicate toys that will permit the youngsters to carry on parallel play at the same time. In this way both children will be satisfied. If you realize that sharing is still beyond the child's comprehension at two, you will be able to prevent needless fussing. A wagon or ball may be left in the playroom to encourage any efforts at cooperative play. The two-year-old is very much of an individual and is primarily interested in handling his play materials and in imitating the play of others.

By the time your child is *three years old*, he will be more mature and ready to take turns and share. His imagination and sense of dramatization will begin to enter into his play and he will be more interested in playing with other children. He will begin to use his blocks to build bridges, houses or garages, and to dramatize these activities with his toys.

At *four*, the child will want to use his play materials more constructively to represent the activities he has seen and enjoyed. Indeed, his ideas will often exceed his own ability to carry them out in detail! The four-year-old is frequently bossy in his play with others and seems to get pleasure in doing things that appear silly to others.

FIRST PLAY CONTACTS

By the time your child is *five*, he will want to finish the things he has begun and his interest in one activity alone may carry over for several days.

A friendly attitude toward the children he comes in contact with in his play will be a real asset in helping your child make satisfying social adjustments.

The rhymes, stories and pictures in My BOOK HOUSE will suggest many activities that your child will want to carry out in his play.

Selections similar to:

Teddy Bear, Teddy Bear (B.H., I:91) suggest activities that the child will like to imitate.

Building with Blocks (B.H., I:164) suggests buildings that he will want to try to make with his own blocks.

The Police Cop Man (B.H., I:173), *Biting Marion* (B.H., I:174), *Train Story* (B.H., I:179), *Mister Postman* (B.H., I:182), and *The Elevator* (B.H., I:183), give him many ideas to carry out with his own toy trains, autos and trucks.

The Snow Man (B.H., I:192), and *Snow* (B.H., II:208) suggest snow activities.

Playing in the Sandpile (B.H., I:195) suggest activities for his sandpile or box.

Paper Boats (B.H., II:139) suggest making paper boats and sailing them in his tub or pond.

The Zoo in the Park (B.H., I:186), *The Orchestra* (B.H., I:187), *The Big Umbrella and the Little Rubbers* (B.H., I:190), *The Teddy Bears' Picnic* (B.H., II:57), *The Circus Parade* (B.H., III:46), *The Swing* (B.H., III:92) and *A Happy Day in the City* (B.H., III:181) all suggest rhythms and dramatic play that will appeal to the child.

Other suggestions for play activities will be found in the Packet of *Creative Work for Your Child's Hands*—Part III of My BOOK HOUSE Plan.

Chapters XVII to XXII of this book give additional helps and suggestions for creative activities that your child will want to carry out in his play.

CHAPTER IX

Expose Your Child to Nature Experiences

PARENTS frequently lose sight of the many opportunities they have to introduce their child to the simple wonders in nature. All too often they are convinced that one must be a naturalist or live in the great outdoors to point out simple happenings the child will enjoy. In reality, whether we live in the crowded city or the quiet of the country, we can observe the sun, moon, stars, wind, rain or snow, and seasonal changes. Every child is curious to know more about the things he sees all around him!

A walk in almost any community will give your child a chance to see trees budding in the spring or getting ready for winter. He can experience, firsthand, the change in the sun, wind and rain as the seasons progress. Plan your walk so there is plenty of time for him to investigate the things you may want to point out, and be careful not to try to crowd too many incidents into one trip.

NATURE EXPERIENCES

The little child will more fully appreciate the shade from trees if he has been allowed to stand in it on a hot day and enjoy the cool refreshment it offers. Do not be disturbed or try to hurry him if he wants to stop to pick up the fuzzy caterpillar or earthworm he has discovered for himself. It is only through these intimate contacts with nature that he will come to understand and appreciate its many mysteries. Before long he will be making many wonderful discoveries of his own and want to share them with you.

Your child's attitude toward nature and the great outdoors, his love and appreciation of bird, animal and plant life, will depend largely upon your own everyday attitude and interest in these same things. Nature offers the parent and child many mutual experiences to further the growth of a fine relationship.

The little child who is familiar with the things in nature found in his own home environment, will be more alert and appreciative of beauty in the world at large. At an early age he learns to know the feel of soil and sand as he mixes and pats mud pies. He learns about the strength of the wind from sailing his own boat on the pond.

Nature Rhymes and Stories Help Child Understand Natural Phenomena. They add to his confidence and security. Poems and stories that tell about the friendly, useful work of the rain will help allay his fears of storms, lightning and thunder. The rain that is keeping him from outdoor play will not seem so hostile if he has heard

55

IN YOUR HANDS

friendly verses similar to,

> *How beautiful is the rain!*
> *After the dust and heat,*
> *In the broad and fiery street,*
> *In the narrow lane,*
> *How beautiful is the rain.*[1]
>
> or
>
> *The rain is raining all around,*
> *It falls on field and tree,*
> *It rains on the umbrellas here,*
> *And on the ships at sea.*[2]

He will discover the rhythm of the rain as it patters on his roof and windowpane. He will find mystery in the wind that is howling through the trees, if he is familiar with verse similar to, ...

> *Who has seen the wind?*
> *Neither you nor I;*
> *But when the trees bow down their heads,*
> *The wind is passing by.*[3]
>
> or
>
> *"Come, little leaves," said the wind one day,*
> *"Come over the meadows with me and play;*
> *Put on your dresses of red and gold,*
> *For summer is gone and the days grow cold."*[4] . . . .

Frequently parents take for granted the child will discover all the interesting things in nature for himself and, as a result, he may be deprived of fascinating experiences. Be careful not to bore your little child with scientific facts beyond his understanding.

[1]How Beautiful Is the Rain—B.H., III:25   [3]Who Has Seen the Wind—B.H., I:201
[2]Rain—B.H., I:191   [4]Come, Little Leaves—B.H., II:70

NATURE EXPERIENCES

Rhymes, stories and pictures about the moon, sun, stars, birds and animals, will help awaken his interest in the familiar things around him and give them more appeal.

A Magnifying Glass Adds Interest to Nature Experiences. It encourages your child to examine the things he sees more closely. Let him save the cocoon he sees on his walk and he is certain to be curious about the caterpillar that spun it, and the beautiful butterfly that will emerge from it. A grasshopper, spider or praying mantis may be kept comfortable in a ventilated jar or box for a few days to give the child a chance to learn more about them. Milkweed pods, nuts, stones, shells or fallen leaves, can well be the start of a nature collection that will bring him a great deal of pleasure. An aquarium where he can study the habits and characteristics of fish, snails, turtles and tadpoles, will delight him. Planting and caring for his own little garden, providing food for birds and pets, and arranging flowers for the table, are but a few of the many other experiences he will enjoy.

Answer the little child's questions in language simple enough for him to understand, and save the more scientific explanations until he is ready to absorb them. As the child's nature experiences broaden, he will feel the need for more detailed knowledge and seek authentic references to satisfy his needs. During this period he may

57

IN YOUR HANDS

put forth tremendous effort to read scientific books on the subject most appealing to him. The child who is able to find interesting things in nature will never be at a loss for a hobby to follow in his leisure time. Experiences with nature are sure to add color and beauty to your child's speech and thinking, and influence his desire to create.

REFERENCES

See Nature selections listed in Index of My BOOK HOUSE, Volume XII, under:

See Nature Experiences and Social Science on various charts — pages 80 to 105 of this book, and Unit No. 5 of *Creative Work for Your Child's Hands.*

Building Number Experiences

CHAPTER X

THE manner in which the little child meets number experiences in the home, before he goes to school, may influence his understanding and liking for mathematics later on. Much of the time allotted to the teaching of numbers in the first three grades is spent in helping the child build up a number vocabulary to interpret terms found in arithmetic problems.

By the time the child is ready to enter first grade, he is expected to know how to count to ten, and to understand the meaning of terms like, *big* and *little*, *long* and *short*, *full* and *empty*, *more than* and *less than*, etc. He is also expected to speak of groups of two or three objects as, *two* cows or *three* birds—without having to stop to count them individually. In other words, the child entering first grade should have formed a *number concept* of two or three objects.

Number Concepts are Formed Early. Reading Readiness Tests are given to children entering first grade in an effort to determine their understanding of numbers. To take these tests, the child

59

must be able to mark certain pictures[1] in a booklet according to directions given by the teacher. One page of the test booklet deals with a group of houses pictured with doors and windows. The child will be asked to, "Put a mark on the house with *three*[2] windows and *one* door."

He will be asked to look at a row of pictures of nests containing eggs, and told to, "Put a mark on the nest with *five*[2] eggs in it."

He will be asked to look at a row of pictures of men, and told to, "Put a mark on the *tallest*[2] one."

The child will be allowed only five seconds to follow each direction and mark the correct picture in his test booklet. If he is to complete the test in the time allowed, he must have some concept of numbers before entering school. If he is unable to immediately identify the picture of two, three or four objects, he will fail in his test, as there is not enough time allowed him to stop and count the individual objects.

[1]Pictures from Reading Readiness Tests for Entering First Grade Pupils, based on the Alice and Jerry books, used by permission of the copyright owners, Row, Peterson and Company, Evanston, Illinois.

[2]See Reference List, page 64 of this book.

NUMBER EXPERIENCES

Rhymes and Stories Add Meaning to Number Words. The little child who has heard number words repeated in conversation, stories and rhymes, will have formed a far greater number concept than the parent realizes. It is not advisable to teach your child merely to *say* numbers. It is very possible for him to repeat numbers perfectly from *one* to *one hundred*, without having learned anything about the relationship of one number to another.

The child's daily routine offers many natural situations for him to gather concrete facts about numbers and their meaning. For example: When the little child hears the nursery rhyme, *Rub-a-dub-dub, three men in a tub* (Volume I, page 48), he will see the picture of the *three* men in a tub at the same time he hears the word *three* mentioned in the rhyme. The word *three* will begin to take on meaning for him as he associates the words he *hears* with the picture he *sees*. In reality, he will begin to form his own concept of meaning for the word and number *three*.

In the humorous New England ballad, *Old Noah* (Volume I, page 112), he will hear many number phrases repeated—" . . . . There's *one* wide river to cross . . . . The animals went in *two* by *two*. The elephant and the kangaroo . . . . " Here again, as the child looks at the picture that tells of the "one wide river" and the "elephant and the kangaroo," going in "two by two," he will begin to associate the meaning of the words with the relationship between *one* and *two*. He sees that two is *more than* one, and likewise, that one is *less than* two.

In Volume II, page 94, you will find another old favorite, *Ten Little Indians*. In this rhyme the child not only hears the names of the numbers from one to ten, but, he also has an opportunity to learn the relationship of one number to another. He will enjoy the humor of the rhyme at the same time he is learning that ten little Indians are *more than* four or five little Indians. The illustrations will add appeal and help him form a concept for the

61

numbers mentioned in the rhyme.

Counting-rhymes and stories interest the child and help give him a number vocabulary that he will use and understand. The child who has number words in his vocabulary will be able to express his ideas more accurately. In the story, *The Three Autos* (Volume I, page 177), he will become familiar with the comparative terms, big, little and enormous, and begin using them in his own conversation.

Everyday Number Experiences. Play experiences offer the child many opportunities to use his knowledge of numbers. The number ex-

periences that come up naturally in the child's day will be the most meaningful to him. Let him be responsible for counting the chairs, plates and napkins needed for the family dinner. Let him discover the number of fingers and toes on his hands and feet, and the number of buttons on his suit, by counting them. Speak of his age and the number of pounds he weighs and you will find him doing likewise. These are but a few experiences that will make numbers more meaningful to him. Encourage him to use terms, such as oldest, youngest, tallest, etc., when he needs them in his conversation. Reading numbers on houses, automobile licenses and the telephone dial; identifying coins, as a penny, nickel, dime, etc.; speaking of his gloves and shoes, as a *pair* of gloves and a *pair* of shoes; and asking the grocer for a *dozen* eggs, a *pound* of butter or a *quart* of milk; will add much to his understanding of numbers. Let him select the *two* cookies he may have in mid-afternoon and the

NUMBER EXPERIENCES

little apple or *big* orange he wants to eat.

When he is a little older, draw his attention to the numbers on the pages of his book. When he is learning to read for himself, encourage him to use the index in his book to find the story he wants. Dominoes, number and counting games where scorekeeping is required, will tend to make his knowledge of numbers more practical and usable. Let him become familiar with the calendar and learn to speak of the days of the week and the names of the months when he has reason to refer to them. Draw his  attention to the dates on letters, newspapers and magazines, and the numbers on thermometers and clocks.

The child learns the value of measuring and planning when he is faced with the problem of making things fit. He learns by experience to choose the correct size of paper or wood that will best suit his needs. In fact, it is amazing how quickly the little child learns to judge size and distance by looking and examining. His conversation will become more specific and accurate as number words seep into his vocabulary.

The child's introduction to numbers will be pleasant or boresome, meaningful or vague, according to the early experiences he is exposed to in the home before he goes to school. In the selections found in the first three volumes of My BOOK HOUSE, he will hear many words and phrases that will help him understand numbers, time, days of the week, seasons, measures, etc.

REFERENCES:

Counting Rhymes, Index, B.H., XII:235
Also:
Diddle, Diddle, Dumpling—B.H., I:37
Old King Cole—B.H., I:44
Rub-a-Dub-Dub—B.H., I:48

IN YOUR HANDS

There Were Two Blackbirds—B.H., I:51
Three Little Kittens—B.H., I:53
There Were Two Little Boys—B.H., I:74
Engine, Engine Number Nine—B.H., I:85
Here Come Three Jolly, Jolly Sailor Boys—B.H., I:96
Three Old Maids A-Skating Went—B.H., I:110
There Were Three Duckies in a Brookie—B.H., I:127
Mary Milks the Cow—B.H., I:135
The Children and the Bear—B.H., I:206

STORIES WITH NUMBER REFERENCES

Reen-Reen-Reeny-Croak-Frog—B.H., II:37
Two Birds and Their Nest—B.H., II:45
The Little Rabbit Who Wanted Red Wings—B.H., II:87
Noah's Ark—B.H., II:101
The Tale of Peter Rabbit—B.H., II:112
Little Black Sambo—B.H., II:118
The Village of Cream Puffs—B.H., II:124
Verses on Kingsley's Water Babies—B.H., III:211

See suggestions for making clay numbers—found on page 157 of this book.

²Typical references to number words and comparative terms appearing in the Reading Readiness Tests, will be found in the following selections in My BOOK HOUSE:

THREE

Old King Cole—Vol. I, page 44
Three Little Kittens—Vol. I, page 53
The Three Autos—Vol. I, page 177
Johnny and the Three Goats—Vol. II, page 47
Goldilocks and the Three Bears—Vol. III, page 20

FIVE

Dame Durden—Vol. I, page 58
Five Little Chicks—Vol. I, page 64
Over in the Meadow—Vol. I, page 138
Ten Little Indians—Vol. II, page 94

NUMBER EXPERIENCES

TALL

See Counting and Number Experiences on charts—pages 80 to 93 of this book.

CHAPTER XI

Encourage Your Child's Natural Readiness for Learning

YOU can make the task of learning easier and more inviting to your child if you encourage his natural readiness for learning with a background of meaningful experiences. Jean Rousseau, a famous French philosopher, once said, "The child has needs of his own and a mind appropriate for those needs."

At Birth the Baby Has a Natural Readiness for Learning. The experiences the parent provides for him will largely determine his ability to adjust himself to the world about him. His home environment and early experiences help set the stage for his mental maturity and readiness for learning. The baby of six months *is not physically ready* to walk and talk, but he *is ready* to sit up by himself and crow and squeal with delight. The *one-year-old* has comparatively few words in his vocabulary, while the *two-year-old is ready* to use three or even four words in phrases and sentences.

The child who is *ready to learn* is *eager to learn*. During his preschool days he must learn many things in order to be happy and comfortable with his friends and playmates. Social adjustment, personal responsibility and human relationships truly begin in babyhood. The wise parent will not wait to *discover* readiness for learning in the child. He will *plan* a rich background of experiences that will add meaning to the child's interpretation of the things around him. Such a background will include a wealth of firsthand and story experiences to encourage language ability, social adjustment, personal responsibility, and a chance to mature fully at each age level. The child should have access to play materials and equipment that give him an opportunity to investigate and create. It is only natural for children to vary in their readiness for learning as their mental and emotional maturity are influenced by the things they experience.

School Programs Planned Around Readiness of Child. They are planned to suit the readiness qualities of the children enrolled. By kindergarten age the child should have formed the *habit of listening* in order that he may be ready to *listen to learn*. The kindergarten program is planned for children who are familiar with creative materials like clay, paint, crayons, etc. It is planned around children who have had a background of rhymes, poems, stories and experiences to help them understand the language of the schoolroom. By kindergarten age, the child should be ready to help himself and act independently. The child who has formed good work habits will be cooperative and courteous in his relationship with other children and *ready* to make his adjustments to new situations with ease.

The child who is *ready to learn* will be able to experience success rather than discouragement and failure. Each new experience your child encounters will be influenced by the preparation he has had to understand and interpret it. If the parent attempts to force learning situations on the child that are beyond his mental maturity and comprehension, he may create a feeling of inferiority and discouragement that will handicap him for further learning. Let your child's mental maturity set his standards for learning and he will be more successful in his first school contacts.

My BOOK HOUSE will encourage your child's natural readiness for learning at each phase in his development. The selections are woven around the child's interests and are on his own level of understanding. Using My BOOK HOUSE Plan in your home will keep you in touch with your child's needs and desires and provide an enriched story and experience background to nurture his mental maturity and readiness to learn. It will enable you to meet your child on his own level of understanding and give him experiences to guide him to happiness and success in his social, mental and emotional adjustments.

See charts on:
What the School Expects of Your Child in Kindergarten—pages 80 to 85 of this book.
What the School Expects of Your Child in Grades One, Two and Three—pages 86 to 93 of this book.

CHAPTER XII

Readiness For Grades One, Two and Three

PSYCHOLOGISTS and educators have set the first three grades in school as the *readiness period for reading.* Learning to read, they agree, should be determined by the child's physical, mental, social and emotional maturity. The experiences he has in the home during the preschool years, then, will determine your child's readiness for the learning expected of him. Wise parents will plan to encourage the child's natural development and readiness for learning from babyhood to school age. Parents are constantly asking, "What can we do to help our child in these early years?" Perhaps this question can be best answered by examining the reasons educators give for failure in the primary grades.

Causes of Failure in the First Three Grades.

1. Inadequate preparation in the home.
2. Meager vocabulary.
3. Inability to pay attention.
4. Entering school with insufficient story background.
5. Lack of desire to read.

It is evident that most of the experiences that promote the child's readiness for learning and reading take place in the home before he enters school. The state and national governments recognize the importance of these early years at home and have set up preschool clinics to secure the cooperation of mothers in making the child's first school experiences more successful. By the time he is ready to enter school the child's personality and attitude toward learning, his habits and character qualities are crystallized in the mold you have fixed for them during his early years at home.

Qualities that Make for Readiness for Learning and Reading in the First Three Grades. These must be developed gradually in your child over a period of time. There is no magic formula for developing them just prior to the time he enters school. If the child is to be ready to learn, he must be able to:

1. Listen and pay attention.

The habit of listening and paying attention should begin in the first few months of baby's life, and his ability to listen, pay attention and concentrate will grow from year to year. In first grade he will be expected to have an attention span of at least fifteen minutes. Learning to listen and pay attention are basic to your child's readiness for learning. Carefully graded rhymes, poems, stories and pictures will appeal to him and make him *want* to listen and pay attention.

2. Reproduce stories in his own words.

The child must hear a variety of rhymes, poems and stories over and over again before he has a desire to retell them. He is interested in talking about familiar things that make up his own world—for these are the things he understands. The child is dependent on you for his literary experiences during the early years. The literary experiences he gains from the rhymes, poems and stories he hears every day, will stimulate his desire to share his experiences with others. These first stories should be written in short well-knit sentences and in a vocabulary suited to his needs. Up until five, he is not interested in plots. Stories like *First Adventures* (Volume I, page 160), *The Three Autos* (Volume I, page 177) etc., are typical experience stories that encourage retelling. Selections with repetitive qualities such as *Over in the Meadow* (Volume I, page 138), *The Little Gray Pony* (Volume II, page 17) and *The Gingerbread Man* (Volume II, page 58), invite the child to repeat familiar parts.

3. *Observe details in objects and pictures.*

Throughout My BOOK HOUSE beautiful illustrations, accurate in every detail, add to the child's enjoyment and give him the necessary preschool preparation. *Little Jack Horner* (Volume I, page 48) actually sits in the corner and the little child can easily tell from the picture illustrating *Rub-a-Dub-Dub* (Volume I, page 48) which is the butcher and which is the baker. Children depend on pictures to interpret the meaning of the stories and it is important that the illustrations in their first books be accurate. Pictures help the child build up the sound and meaning of many new words. For example, the poems at the top of page 86 in Volume I,

Star light, star bright,
Very first star I've seen tonight;.....

deals with "one star" and the illustration accompanying it has emphasized this thought with one star pictured in the sky. The second poem,

Many, many stars are in the skies
As old, as old as Adam;..........

emphasizes the phrase "many stars" and so the illustration accompanying it shows the sky filled with stars. The words of these poems and the illustrations *belong together* and help the child *see* what he *hears* and *reads*. In this way he builds concepts of the new words he hears and is unconsciously being prepared for reading.

71

4. *Express his ideas and share them with the group.*

In order to do this with confidence he must have a vocabulary of about 3000 words and be able to enunciate clearly. The child who is familiar with the selections in the first three volumes in My BOOK HOUSE has been exposed to 6800 different words used over and over again to express a variety of ideas, and it is only natural to assume that he will use many of these in his own speech.

5. *Understand and use comparative terms.*

A story background will help him develop his ability along this line. My BOOK HOUSE provides for this phase in his development by including hundreds of comparative terms like,

big	fast	near	dark	cool	more than
little	slow	far	light	warm	less than
enormous					

6. *Follow directions.*

The child with a good understanding and speaking vocabulary is equipped to understand and follow directions with ease and confidence. My BOOK HOUSE Plan helps your child build an understanding and speaking vocabulary, form the habit of listening and paying attention, think through situations, and act with confidence.

The parent in the home has the ideal situation for building a love and desire for reading. A story is a very intimate experience to the little child and so he wants to be close to the person who reads to him. In school he rarely has the opportunity to sit beside the person who reads to the group. A background of stories will give your child many experiences that would otherwise be denied him. Stories and poems add interest and meaning to his everyday happenings and supply many details that he overlooks in familiar situations. Your child is entitled to the best literature available and My BOOK HOUSE brings it right into your own home.

Long stories will tire the little child and develop the habit of inattention rather than the habit of listening and paying attention. The stories he hears in his preschool years must be free from complicated plots, and the language and sentence structure simple enough to make him want to use the words and phrases in his own daily speech. Stories will help your child mature more fully at each age level in his development and so they must cover a variety of childhood interests. Many children are deprived of happy experiences in literature when parents choose only animal or train stories and exclude rhymes, poems and stories of everyday activities, nature, community interests, the Bible, wholesome adventure and imaginative interests, as well as story friends from other lands. Carefully graded stories on your child's own level of understanding suggest desirable social qualities that he automatically accepts as his own. They enable him to make decisions of his own and help him gain a better understanding of honesty, truth, kindness and courtesy.

Reading Difficulties in Primary Grades. Limited story and language experiences cause reading failures. Do not overlook the value of a story background to encourage your child's readiness for learning. He will never forget the stories you have taken the time to read to him. Down through the years he will treasure the memory of the person who read them and place his first story friends on a cherished list. If you want to stimulate your child's desire to read for himself, make story time a happy intimate experience in his day.

See charts on:
What the School Expects of Your Child in Kindergarten—pages 80 to 85 of this book.
What the School Expects of Your Child in Grades One, Two and Three—pages 86 to 93 of this book.

CHAPTER XIII

When the Child Reads for Himself
Grades Four, Five and Six

BY the time the child enters fourth grade the school expects him to have mastered the basic techniques of reading and be ready to read widely for study, information and enjoyment.

It is usually about this period in the child's development that many parents lose contact with his reading interests and let him shift for himself. It is also at this very same period that the child is faced with reading problems too difficult for him to solve alone. Although he has learned to read fairly well, he still needs your help to select his reading. His interests have grown in leaps and bounds and his quest for information has frequently grown beyond his own reading ability. It is much wiser, then, to use this opportunity to guide your child's *choice* of reading in order that he will continue to choose reading for recreation and pleasure.

Choose Material on Child's Level of Understanding. The child of nine or ten frequently has difficulty finding interesting and satisfying reading material outside the schoolroom. If he is left to struggle with reading too difficult, he may lose interest in it and look upon it only as a necessary evil for study in school.

You will find My BOOK HOUSE a valuable aid in guiding your child's choice of reading during this transitional stage. It will give him interesting and enjoyable reading in his own home that is vital to his natural development. And, what is most important, the selections he reads will be graded to suit his reading ability as well as his interests. He will come to identify the literature he reads as nature, fanciful, realistic and factual stories, and speak of other selections as myths, legends, folk tales, epics and biographies. He will become familiar with the work of the outstanding poets and identify selections as belonging to periods in the history of literature. He will be exposed to a balanced variety of reading material including stories from the Bible, selections from Shakespeare and Chaucer, and outstanding characters in history, science and the arts. The selections he reads will develop his appreciation of good literature and make him more discriminating in his reading. The notes at the bottom of the pages in My BOOK HOUSE volumes suggest additional books for him to read and he will feel pride in his ability to ask the librarian for these by title and author. During this period the child begins to develop special tastes in reading and it is most important that he be exposed to a variety of good literature in order that he may choose wisely.

In My BOOK HOUSE your child will have the opportunity to read selections from the literature of the world and gain valuable information in which to clothe the facts of history, geography and social science that he is accumulating in school. He will gather ideas that will add interest and life to his studies. The child's love for adventure is high during this period and My BOOK HOUSE selections will provide him with tales of heroes and adventurers who have contributed to our civilization. During this period your child's social behavior and choice of language will reflect his attempt to imitate the people he admires. The characters he meets in his reading will unconsciously influence his own emotional reactions and social behavior.

See charts on What the School Expects of Your Child in Grades Four, Five and Six on pages 94 to 99 of this book.

CHAPTER XIV

Reading in the Upper Grades

READING must provide pleasure, relaxation and growth to satisfy the boy or girl in the upper grades and junior high school. The child's capacity for understanding what he reads and his ability to read fluently grow with each new reading and personal experience. During these years, his appreciation for literature and quest for pleasurable and discriminating reading will depend upon the background of stories parents and teachers have given him.

The literature he seeks must stir his emotions and portray life in such a manner that he will be able to link it with his own. It should give him an opportunity to experience the author's reactions, and bring him in contact with characters whose personalities and experiences will enrich his thoughts and ideas.

Share Your Child's Reading Interests. For the most part, parents overestimate the reading ability and maturity of the child in the upper grades. The early adolescent's span of attention is comparatively brief. Short stories, prose selections and abridged novels are better suited to his needs than the full length book. How often the child of this age confesses to parent, teacher and friend that he has read a book but was unable to get any sense out of it! The child's appreciation of literature develops gradually from early childhood through adolescence. Take advantage of every opportunity to share in your child's reading activities. The parent who reads certain exciting chapters and outstanding scenes aloud will add pleasure and interest to the child's reading and encourage him to read the selections for himself.

Reading Influences Personality Development. The style of literature

76

UPPER GRADES

your child comes in contact with will influence his personality, conversation and attempts at writing. His style and pattern of thinking, talking and writing is largely a matter of imitation and reflects the type of literature he hears and reads. John Bunyan and Abraham Lincoln are but two proofs of the influence of reading in the formation of style, character and personality. The Bible was the dominant source of their reading. Bunyan's *Pilgrim's Progress* and Lincoln's speeches and addresses plainly reveal the simplicity, directness and appeal of this "Book of Books."

These are the years for your boy or girl to meet Dickens, Clemens, Hawthorne, Irving, Shakespeare and other fine literary personalities. Biographies that trace the human struggles and conflicts of artists, musicians, authors, explorers, statesmen and scientists, will inspire and encourage the adolescent to read widely. Bible and hero stories, tales of chivalry, adventure and romance also have strong appeal. At this age, the child is interested in dramatization, making scenery and costumes for plays and marionette shows, and reads avidly for details to help him reproduce them realistically.

Importance of Varied Reading. During the later school years the child is called upon to do many types of reading. He must know how to skim for facts, read in detail for description, be able to pick essential points from his reading for history, as well as evaluate the material he has read. A varied background of reading will tend to make him more efficient in his studies. Isolated facts are not as meaningful or retained as easily by him as information he gleans from authentic story material. For instance, in the biography of Henry Wadsworth Longfellow, called *The Harvard Professor* (Volume XII, page 135), the youthful reader not only gathers factual material about the great poet, but, at the same time, meets outstanding poets and authors of Longfellow's day. In this same selection, he meets Ralph Waldo Emerson, Nathaniel Hawthorne,

IN YOUR HANDS

Oliver Wendell Holmes, James Russell Lowell, Henry Thoreau and John Greenleaf Whittier, as friends of Longfellow. How much easier it will be for him to identify the New England writers he is studying at school after this reading experience! The story element gives him facts in their proper setting and makes them more appealing and meaningful. Do not overlook the need for poetry and prose at this age as the musical sound of words holds particular charm for the adolescent.

My BOOK HOUSE provides your child with a balanced variety of literature that he will understand and enjoy. Begin in his early years to build his love and appreciation for literature and he will enter into adolescence with a natural desire to read, the ability to discriminate, and a taste for literature.

A wide variety of selections from the literature of the world are listed in the Index of My BOOK HOUSE, Volume XII, under the following headings:

The child using this Index will get valuable experience that will help him to classify the various periods in literature. He will learn to associate the authors, poets and playwrights with the correct country, period and literary group. Reading experiences similar to these will add meaning and interest to his study of literature in school and make it more inviting.

See charts for Grades Seven, Eight and Nine—pages 100 to 105 of this book.

CHAPTER XV

Home-School Coordinating Charts

The charts on the following pages have been prepared for parents who are using My BOOK HOUSE. The first chart gives a comprehensive picture of the attitudes and qualities that must be developed in the preschool child if he is to make a happy, successful adjustment to the new environment of the schoolroom. The right-hand page of the chart lists the material in My BOOK HOUSE that will help develop the necessary habits and attitudes in the child.

The next three charts reveal to the parent WHAT THE SCHOOL EXPECTS OF THE CHILD from first grade through the upper grades, and indicate WHERE TO FIND HELP IN My BOOK HOUSE Plan. The general aims listed on these charts for each grade in school have been chosen after a careful digest of the courses of study used in schools throughout the United States. With this information at hand the parent will be better equipped to understand the child's needs and offer intelligent guidance.

It is more important for the parent to provide a home background that will enrich the child's experiences, stimulate his imagination and arouse his intellectual curiosity, than to drill him on the things he is learning at school or help him with his actual lessons. Play equipment, creative materials such as clay, paint, crayons, etc., and carefully selected books in the home will encourage the child's natural readiness for learning. The child's attitude toward school will reflect his parents' attitude toward reading, learning and problem-solving, just as his speech reflects the language he hears in the home.

The aims of both home and school must be coordinated if the child is to enjoy a full life and make his adjustments happily and successfully.

IN YOUR HANDS

What the School Expects of Your Child
In Kindergarten

SOCIAL BEHAVIOR AND ADJUSTMENT QUALITIES	To show self-control and self-dependence. To exhibit fairness in work and play. To lead graciously and follow willingly. To be courteous in his speech and actions. To appreciate the work of others. To be relaxed and at ease with the group.

LANGUAGE AND LITERATURE ACTIVITIES	To retell short stories and learn rhymes and poems. To create stories and verse. To engage wholeheartedly in dramatic and imaginative play. To share ideas with others and contribute to group discussions. To speak in complete sentences and enunciate clearly. To follow directions and understand the language of the schoolroom.

HOME-SCHOOL CHARTS

Where to Find Help In My BOOK HOUSE
In Kindergarten

See chapters V and XVI of this book.
See selections listed in Index of My BOOK HOUSE, Volume XII, under:

Choose stories best suited to your child's needs and level of understanding.

See chapters II, III, and XI of this book.

My BOOK HOUSE selections stimulate the child's desire to retell his story experiences and to share his ideas with others. They also encourage his love of good language and give him language patterns he unconsciously imitates in his own conversation.

Experience stories about everyday happenings expose him to short well-knit sentences to use in his own speech.

See selections listed in Index of My BOOK HOUSE, Volume XII, under:

Repetitive selections—
Volume I, pages 33, 38, 102, 110, 112, 114, 126, 138, 160, etc.
Volume II, pages 13, 17, 47, 52, 58, 118, 145, 192, 200, 209
Volume III, pages 76, 85, 99, 111

The colorful accurate pictures accompanying the selections in My BOOK HOUSE help the child *see* what he *hears* and build concepts of meaning for new words.

The child in kindergarten is expected to have a speaking and understanding vocabulary of 3500 to 4000 words. In the selections in the first three volumes of My BOOK HOUSE, he hears over 6800 different words which will help enrich his own vocabulary.

IN YOUR HANDS

What the School Expects of Your Child
In Kindergarten

CREATIVE EXPRESSION

To experiment freely with scissors, paper, paste, clay, paint, wood, cloth, crayon, etc., in a constructive way.

To use sand, blocks, playground equipment, etc., constructively.

To be imaginative and to express a variety of ideas with creative materials.

To choose his own activities and have a desire to reproduce individual experiences.

To be resourceful in use of materials.

To recognize and name colors.

COUNTING AND NUMBER EXPERIENCES

To use numbers in work and play.

To include number words in vocabulary when needed.

To be able to count to 10 and know something of the relationship of one number to another.

NATURE EXPERIENCES AND SOCIAL SCIENCE

To be conscious of beauty and happenings in nature.

To be kind and considerate in care of pets and birds.

To appreciate beauty and care of flowers, plants and trees.

To learn about farm animals and how they help man.

To learn how sun, moon, wind, rain and snow help man.

To recognize and speak of living creatures in his environment, such as birds, animals, insects, etc.

To recognize seasonal changes in wind, sun, trees, etc.

To understand the farmer's contribution toward feeding and clothing man.

HOME·SCHOOL CHARTS

Where to Find Help In My BOOK HOUSE
In Kindergarten

See chapters XVII, XVIII, XIX, and XX of this book.

See Index, Volume XII of My BOOK HOUSE—Creative Activities, page 283.

The Packet of *Creative Work for Your Child's Hands* contains suggestions and detailed instructions for activities encountered in the schoolroom. It gives the child ideas to share with classmates and helps him excel in his work.

Colorful pictures throughout My BOOK HOUSE make the child conscious of color. Names of colors are mentioned in rhymes and stories to connect them with the pictures. (There are nearly 200 references to color in the first three volumes alone.)

Color words are emphasized in the following selections in My BOOK HOUSE:

Volume I, pages 18, 20, 24, 25, 28, 29, 30, 33, 35, 37, 40, 41, etc.

Volume II, pages 13, 17, 23, 24, 26, 30, 33, 35, 37, 40, 41, 45, etc.

See chapter X of this book.

My BOOK HOUSE contains over 175 selections that include number and comparative terms to help the child build a concept of meaning for numbers and their relationship.

The accurate pictures illustrating counting rhymes and stories help the child build a meaningful concept of numbers from 1 to 10; e.g.,

Over in the Meadow (Volume I, page 138)

Ten Little Indians (Volume II, page 94)

See Counting Rhymes in Index of My BOOK HOUSE, Volume XII, page 235 and suggestions for making clay numbers—page 157 of this book.

See chapter IX of this book.

There are over 500 selections in My BOOK HOUSE to awaken your child's interest in nature.

See selections listed in Index of My BOOK HOUSE, Volume XII, under Nature, page 257. (89 species of Animals and 60 species of Birds are listed.)

IN YOUR HANDS

What the School Expects of Your Child

In Kindergarten

DESIRABLE WORK HABITS	To be able to work with a purpose in mind and find satisfaction in his own achievements. To be able to concentrate and have an attention span of at least 15 minutes. To complete work started. To be able to work well alone and with others. To choose materials best suited to his needs. To be able to take care of materials and use them constructively.

MUSIC	To match tones and sing simple melodies. To march, skip, hop and jump in rhythmic fashion. To reproduce simple rhythm on drum, tambourine, rhythm sticks, etc.

HOME-SCHOOL CHARTS

Where to Find Help In My BOOK HOUSE
In Kindergarten

See chapters V and XVII, of this book.

See selections listed in Index of My BOOK HOUSE, Volume XII, under:

Choose selections best suited to your child's needs and level of understanding.

See chapter XXIII of this book.

See selections listed under Music in Index of My BOOK HOUSE, Volume XII, page 254. Interesting stories and notes of over 60 composers from the 17th Century through the Modern Period are included.

Illustrations of musical instruments are listed in the Index of My BOOK HOUSE, Volume XII, page 257.

Suggested stories for kindergarten:

Detailed instructions for making homemade musical instruments are given in the Packet of *Creative Work for Your Child's Hands*.

IN YOUR HANDS

What the School Expects of Your Child
In Grades One, Two and Three

SOCIAL BEHAVIOR AND ADJUSTMENT QUALITIES

To be able to live peaceably with others.
To be cooperative, courteous, considerate and appreciative.
To have good emotional control.
To be helpful and friendly, and respect property of others.
To be truthful and honest, and feel joy in helping others.
To be eager, alert, observing and able to initiate ideas.
To give and take constructive criticism cheerfully.
To assume responsibility, be resourceful and help himself.

LANGUAGE AND LITERATURE ACTIVITIES

To retell stories interestingly in well-knit sentences.
To develop pride in the use of good language.
To enunciate clearly and build an interesting vocabulary.
To understand the language of the schoolroom, follow directions, and share ideas with others.
To have a background of rhymes, stories and poems.
To write original poems, riddles and stories.

HOME-SCHOOL CHARTS

Where to Find Help In My BOOK HOUSE
For Grades One, Two and Three[1]

See chapter V of this book.

See selections listed in Index of My BOOK HOUSE, Volume XII, under:

Choose selections best suited to your child's needs and level of understanding.

See chapters II, III, XI and XII of this book.

The balanced variety of carefully graded selections in My BOOK HOUSE stimulate the child's desire to retell stories and experiences. They also suggest good language patterns which he will use in his own conversation.

The story language of the literature in My BOOK HOUSE builds the child's appreciation for good speech.

See Index of My BOOK HOUSE, Volume XII, for selections that will appeal to your child.

For Repetitive selections see Reading Chart on page 91 of this book.

The accurate pictures illustrating the selections make the child familiar with the sound and meaning of many new words.

The selections in My BOOK HOUSE enrich the child's vocabulary. In the first three volumes he hears 6800 different words used in a variety of selections.

[1]See Language and Literature Activities on Kindergarten charts—page 80 of this book.
See Climbing the Ladder of Years—pages 120 to 124 of this book.

IN YOUR HANDS

What the School Expects of Your Child
In Grades One, Two and Three

CREATIVE EXPRESSION

To be able to use materials constructively and express ideas with blocks, clay, paper, wood, crayon, paint, scissors, cloth, etc.

To use saw, hammer, chisel, nails, woodwork table, etc.

To make puppet shows, puppets, stage scenery, costumes, posters, friezes, designs, patterns, etc., for units of study, dramatic play, holidays, gifts, etc.

COUNTING AND NUMBER EXPERIENCES

To build a concept of meaning for numbers and their relationship.

To count by 2's, 3's, 5's and 10's.

To make change and identify coins—toy and real money.

To write numbers.

To read numbers on calendars, charts, timetables, pages of books and in tables of contents of books.

To play games involving counting and scorekeeping.

To know meaning of number terms—one dozen, half dozen, pound, inch, foot, yard, length, height, width, circle, square, rectangle, triangle, pint, quart, gallon, cup and glass.

To solve daily problems involving money and measuring.

To tell sizes of stockings, gloves, shoes, dresses, hats, etc.

To use ruler—1″ markings in 1st grade, ½″ in 2nd grade, and ¼″ in 3rd grade.

DESIRABLE WORK HABITS

To use materials and tools constructively.

To plan before he acts, choose materials wisely, finish one job before starting another, and be orderly and neat.

To show initiative, resourcefulness, pride in workmanship.

To assume responsibility toward work and feel the joy of accomplishment.

To concentrate, cooperate and be courteous and helpful.

To be appreciative and respect the work and skill of others.

HOME-SCHOOL CHARTS

Where to Find Help In My BOOK HOUSE
For Grades One, Two and Three

See chapters XVII, XVIII, XIX, and XX of this book.

See Index, Volume XII of My BOOK HOUSE—Creative Activities, page 283.

The Packet of *Creative Work for Your Child's Hands* contains suggestions and detailed instructions for activities encountered in the schoolroom. It gives the child ideas to share with classmates and helps him excel in his work.

Throughout the twelve volumes of My BOOK HOUSE the child finds suggestions and ideas to stimulate his desire to create.

See chapter X of this book.

My BOOK HOUSE contains over 175 selections that include number and comparative terms to help the child build a concept of meaning for numbers and their relationship.

References to numbers are found in the following selections in My BOOK HOUSE:

Volume I, pages 19, 39, 43, 44, 47, 48, 49, 51, 53, 54, 55, 57, 58, 60, 100, 110, 112, 121, 127, 135, 138, 156, 177, etc.

Volume II, pages 24, 25, 33, 45, 47, 87, 94, 96, 101, 112, 118, 124, etc.

Volume III, pages 12, 20, 28, 76, 95, 110, 111, 129, 204, etc.

See Counting Rhymes in Index of My BOOK HOUSE, Volume XII, page 235.

See suggestions for making clay numbers on page 157 of this book.

See chapters V and XVII of this book.

See selections listed in Index of My BOOK HOUSE, Volume XII, under:

Choose selections best suited to your child's needs and level of understanding.

IN   YOUR   HANDS

What the School Expects of Your Child
In Grades One, Two and Three

MUSIC

To appreciate music and enjoy expressing himself in song.

To originate steps to rhythm and play singing games.

To learn about time, notes and tone values.

To sing on pitch, match tones and carry tunes.

To listen to music and identify two or three instruments.

To recognize at least six compositions and name the composers.

To make simple homemade instruments, learn the scale, and originate tunes.

READING

To enjoy reading and get thought from the printed page.

To learn to sound new words quickly and read aloud without stopping before individual words.

To read poetry and prose orally with good expression.

To be able to locate simple passages in books of his own reading ability.

To be able to answer thought questions through reading.

To learn to grasp main ideas when reading silently.

To develop study habits and a reasonable oral and silent reading speed.

To learn to sense a phrase or line before reading aloud.

To cover a great deal of easy reading material and seek outside reading to help develop fluency.

Reading Vocabulary for Grades One, Two and Three

To develop a reading vocabulary in

Grade One—of from 1000 to 2000 words.

Grade Two—of from 1500 to 3000 words.

Grade Three—of from 2500 to 4000 words.

HOME-SCHOOL CHARTS

Where to Find Help In My BOOK HOUSE
For Grades One, Two and Three

See chapter XXIII of this book.

See selections listed under Music in Index of My BOOK HOUSE, Volume XII, page 254. Interesting stories and notes of over 60 composers from the 17th Century through the Modern Period are included.

Illustrations of musical instruments are listed in the Index of My BOOK HOUSE, Volume XII, page 257.

Suggested reading for grades one, two and three:

Volume II, pages 17, 40, 41, 57, 131, 143, 150, 180, 218
Volume III, pages 40, 61, 95, 110, 123, 134, 148, 151, 170
Volume IV, page 159; Volume V, pages 20, 206, 222; Volume VI, page 11

Detailed instructions for making homemade musical instruments are given in the Packet of *Creative Work for Your Child's Hands.*

See chapter XII of this book.
Suggested reading for early school years.
Selections are listed in Index of My BOOK HOUSE, Volume XII, under:

Animals........p. 257   Fables..........p. 242   Humorous
Birds..........p. 262   Fairy Tales.....p. 243   Rhymes and
Boats..........p. 279   Farm and   Stories.......p. 249
City...........p. 233   Country......p. 243   Insects.........p. 265
Experience   Folk Tales and   Lullabies.......p. 256
   Stories and   Legends......p. 244   Mother Goose...p. 254
   Poems........p. 242   Holidays.......p. 248   Nature.........p. 257
                                                   Seasons........p. 267

Choose selections in My BOOK HOUSE best suited to your child's needs and level of understanding.

Repetitive selections: Volume I, pages 33, 38, 102, 110, 112, 114, 126, 138, 160, etc; Volume II, pages 13, 17, 47, 52, 58, 118, 145, 192, 200, 209; Volume III, pages 76, 85, 99, 111.

Parents can stimulate reading interest during this period by continuing to read stories aloud to the child that are beyond his own reading ability.

Reading
Vocabulary in
My BOOK
HOUSE

The selections in the first three volumes of My BOOK HOUSE bring the child in contact with 6800 different words to help him meet the 2500 to 4000 word reading vocabulary required of him in school at the end of third grade.

IN YOUR HANDS

What the School Expects of Your Child

In Grades One, Two and Three

NATURE EXPERIENCES AND SOCIAL SCIENCE

To appreciate nature and be observant of seasonal changes.

To build a concept of meaning for words found in nature and science reading—lake, river, ocean, hill, valley, mountain, climate, temperature, steam, electricity, etc.

To learn sources and use of plants, trees, flowers, fruits, vegetables and animals.

To classify animals as farm, wild, land, water and domestic.

To learn about pets and birds and their use and care.

To learn the part the sun, moon, stars, rain, wind and snow play in life.

To learn sources of food and clothing.

To learn about the work of man—his occupations.

To become familiar with people of the world through poems, stories and pictures.

HOME-SCHOOL CHARTS

Where to Find Help In My BOOK HOUSE
For Grades One, Two and Three

See chapter IX of this book.

There are over 500 selections in My BOOK HOUSE to awaken your child's interest, observation and appreciation of birds, animals, and the beauty of nature. See selections listed in Index of My BOOK HOUSE, Volume XII, under:

Nature, page 257
    Seasons—(53 references listed)
    Lake, Mountain, River, Sea, etc.
    Animals—(89 species listed alphabetically)
    Birds—(60 species of birds are listed)
    Moon, Stars, Sun, Wind, etc.
Occupations, page 268 (32 occupations are listed)
Countries of the World, page 235

IN YOUR HANDS

What the School Expects of Your Child
In Grades Four, Five and Six

**SOCIAL
BEHAVIOR**
To make decisions and have ideas of right and wrong.
To respect authority and the rights of others.
To develop desirable social qualities such as cheerfulness, co-operation, courage, friendliness, generosity, gratitude, happiness, helpfulness, honesty, industry, kindness, leadership, perseverance, politeness, self-control, tolerance, trustworthiness and truthfulness.

MUSIC
To sing for enjoyment.
To read notes of the scale and sing two-part songs.
To develop an appreciation for good music through listening.
To learn about famous composers and their compositions.

HOME-SCHOOL CHARTS

Where to Find Help in My BOOK HOUSE
For Grades Four, Five and Six[1]

See chapter V of this book.

See selections listed in Index of My BOOK HOUSE, Volume XII, under:

Choose selections best suited to your child's needs and level of understanding.

See list of My BOOK HOUSE Selections for Encouraging Dramatic Play in Your Child—page 186 of this book.

See selections listed under Music in Index of My BOOK HOUSE, Volume XII, page 254. Interesting stories and notes of over 60 composers from the 17th Century through the Modern Period are included.

Illustrations of musical instruments are listed in the Index of My BOOK HOUSE, Volume XII, page 257.

Suggested reading in My BOOK HOUSE for grades four, five and six:

Detailed instructions for making homemade musical instruments are given in the Packet of *Creative Work for Your Child's Hands.*

[1]See Music charts for Grades One, Two and Three—pages 90-91 of this book.
See Climbing the Ladder of Years, Your Child's Seventh, Eighth and Ninth Years—page 125 of this book.

**READING,
LANGUAGE
AND
LITERATURE
ACTIVITIES**

To read widely for enjoyment and entertainment.
To gain rich and varied experiences from extensive reading.
To develop fluent oral reading and rapid silent reading.
To follow printed directions and determine central ideas.
To use index, table of contents, dictionary and reference books.
To scan informational reading material at a rapid rate and get the important data and topic information.
To dramatize and illustrate stories.
To do literary reading and social science reading.
To develop desirable study habits.
To gather a background of myths, legends, folk tales, etc., from his reading.
To be able to outline and summarize.

*Reading
Vocabulary
for Grades
Four, Five
and Six*

To develop a reading vocabulary in
    Grade Four—of from 2500 to 4800 words.
    Grade Five—of from 2750 to 5400 words.
    Grade Six—of from 3000 to 5900 words.

**SOCIAL
SCIENCE**

To study the countries of Canada, Mexico and Central America.
To study the sections and possessions of the United States.
To develop a knowledge and appreciation of the relationship between man and environment and trace one region's dependency upon another.
To have the ability to interpret geographical materials.
To make murals and maps.

HOME-SCHOOL CHARTS

Where to Find Help in My BOOK HOUSE
For Grades Four, Five and Six—Continued

See chapter XIII of this book.

For stories suitable for dramatization see list of Selections in My BOOK HOUSE—page 186 of this book.

The child gains an extensive reading background from selections such as those found in My BOOK HOUSE:

My BOOK HOUSE provides unusual reading to share with friends and classmates.

Each volume of My BOOK HOUSE has its own table of contents and Volume XII contains a cross-reference index to give the child additional experience in locating selections.

The story element running through the selections helps impress the important facts on the child's mind and adds interest to his studies.

My BOOK HOUSE selections introduce the child to myths, legends, folk tales and biographies. See selections listed in Index of My BOOK HOUSE, Volume XII, under:

The child comes in contact with many new words in My BOOK HOUSE reading that will enrich his reading vocabulary.

See selections listed in Index of My BOOK HOUSE, Volume XII, under:

IN YOUR HANDS

What the School Expects of Your Child
In Grades Four, Five and Six—Continued

HISTORY

To develop ideals of patriotism and service through an appreciation of racial contributions.

To develop ability to think critically about social questions.

To learn about discoveries, exploration and colonization.

SCIENCE

To develop a scientific attitude.

To develop a knowledge of the world he sees.

To make intelligent adjustments to this world.

To study units of animals, insects, plants, weather and the universe.

POETRY

To commit favorite poems to memory and read poetry for enjoyment.

To study incidental poems.

To memorize ten poems.

To be familiar with poetry of Whittier, Emerson, Longfellow, Morris and Bryant.

HOME-SCHOOL CHARTS

Where to Find Help in My BOOK HOUSE
For Grades Four, Five and Six—Continued

See selections dealing with heroes, patriots and famous characters in history listed in Index of My BOOK HOUSE, Volume XII, under:

Ambition-Leadership.......p. 284   Patriotism................p. 288
Hero and Heroine Stories...p. 247   Countries of the World.....p. 235

Suggested reading in My BOOK HOUSE to help child build a background of history:

      Volume IV, pages 161, 183, 193, 211, 213   Volume VIII, page 82
      Volume V, pages 54, 112, 116, 129, 137

See chapter IX of this book.
See selections in My BOOK HOUSE touching on the discovery of steam, invention of steamboat, etc.

Suggested reading:

      Volume V, pages 45, 48, 66   Volume VI, pages 164, 184

See selections listed in Index of My BOOK HOUSE, Volume XII, under:

Animals.................page 257   Nature..................page 257
Birds...................page 262   Seasons................page 267

In My BOOK HOUSE the child meets the poetry of Whittier, Emerson, Longfellow, Bryant, Noyes, Browning, Shakespeare, Milton, Lindsay, Tennyson, Scott, Rossetti, Burns, Chaucer, etc., as well as psalms from the Bible.

Suggested poetry in My BOOK HOUSE for child in grades four, five and six:

      Volume I, pages 113, 118, 148, 181, 194, 216, 218
      Volume II, pages 78, 79, 105, 140, 141, 152, 163
      Volume III, pages 11, 26, 28, 40, 61, 62, 114, 127, 136, 150, 170, 196, 197, 211
      Volume IV, pages 11, 56, 81, 103, 136, 180, 211
      Volume V, pages 53, 66, 76, 112, 113, 115, 128, 139
      Volume VI, pages 18, 25, 34, 70, 96, 97, 131, 170, 224
      Volume VII, pages 47, 71, 72, 74, 95, 158, 159
      Volume VIII, pages 7, 36, 91, 188
      Volume IX, pages 39, 89, 171
      Volume X, pages 19, 79
      Volume XI, page 7

Foreign rhymes are listed under Countries of the World in Index of My BOOK HOUSE, Volume XII, page 235.

See selections listed in Index of My BOOK HOUSE, Volume XII, under:

      Biographical Sketches, page 230   Nature, page 257
      Countries of the World, page 235   Transportation, page 278

IN YOUR HANDS

What the School Expects of Your Child
In Grades Seven, Eight and Nine

LITERATURE AND LANGUAGE ACTIVITIES

To gain increased enjoyment from reading and appreciate material read.

To increase reading ability, scope of reading and enrich vocabulary.

To have a broader horizon and appreciate description, humor and character.

To read for information.

To write book reviews and give oral reports of books read outside classroom.

To write dramatizations correlated with literature.

To read biographies and factual and travel tales.

To write compositions and descriptive paragraphs and strive for smoothness and originality.

To read Elizabethan Period and Early American Literature, historic tales, Bible stories, romantic poetry and medieval tales.

To read selections by Stevenson, Coleridge, Arnold, Tennyson, Harte, Elliot, Shakespeare, Dickens, Irving, Scott and Cooper.

To develop an appreciation for lovely poems and a desire to commit favorites to memory.

To read narrative poetry.

HOME-SCHOOL CHARTS

Where to Find Help in My BOOK HOUSE
For Grades Seven, Eight and Nine

See chapters III and XIV of this book.

In these grades, the child's outside reading should enrich his studies in school and give him a broader horizon. It should satisfy his craving for travel and adventure.

Diversified reading in My BOOK HOUSE—tales with historical background, literature from Elizabethan and Early American periods, Shakespeare's plays, stories of travel and adventure, Bible stories and medieval tales will develop the child's appreciation of literature and cause him to be more discriminating in his leisure reading. What he reads now will determine to a great extent the pleasure and value he gets from advanced courses in literature and history.

Increased reading ability and an enriched vocabulary will result from reading selections in My BOOK HOUSE listed below:

Volume I, pages 148, 149, 209
Volume II, pages 45, 217
Volume III, page 25
Volume IV, page 212
Volume V, pages 115, 182
Volume VI, pages 36, 146, 213, 224
Volume VII, pages 11, 71, 73, 144, 171, 182, 210
Volume VIII, pages 18, 189
Volume IX, pages 89, 129, 134, 171
Volume X, pages 8, 48, 54, 98, 108, 151, 165, 175, 188, 203, 217, 228
Volume XI, pages 8, 29, 49, 72, 90, 107, 152
Volume XII, pages 15, 30, 36, 42, 66, 74, 94, 102, 104, 108, 110, 113, 116, 118, 120, 122, 135, 143, 147, 154, 163, 190, 213, 221

See also selections listed in Index of My BOOK HOUSE, Volume XII, under:

Biographical Sketches......p. 230   Folk Tales and Legends.....p. 244
Epics....................p. 242   Hero and Heroine Stories...p. 247

The stories in My BOOK HOUSE suggest ideas for dramatization and bring additional interest to your child's studies.

See charts for Grades Four, Five and Six—page 94 of this book.
See Climbing the Ladder of Years, Twelve to Fourteen—page 137 of this book.

IN YOUR HANDS

What the School Expects of Your Child
In Grades Seven, Eight and Nine—Continued

CITIZENSHIP To live peaceably with others and to respect authority.

To develop qualities of courage, cooperation, honesty, industry, initiative, leadership, loyalty, perseverance, resourcefulness, sense of responsibility, self-reliance, tolerance, intelligent "fellowship" which make for good citizenship and successful adjustments to society.

To take an active part in school activities such as student council, assembly programs, safety and health committees.

To make decisions, act independently and seek worthwhile companions.

To utilize leisure time wisely and continue an interest in hobbies.

To develop an understanding of races other than his own.

To encourage a growth of intellectual curiosity.

To compete and match his skill with others of his own age.

SOCIAL STUDIES To study the regions in our own country.

To learn something about the civilizations of China and Japan.

To study the contributions of the early men in science.

To learn about birds and migration.

To study the stars, planets and map-making.

To help understand and interpret facts of his own environment— weather, heat, light, electricity, magnetism, stars, rocks, soil, nature.

To learn about food, care of the body and health.

HOME-SCHOOL CHARTS

Where to Find Help in My BOOK HOUSE

For Grades Seven, Eight and Nine—Continued

See chapter V of this book.

My BOOK HOUSE supplies thrilling stories of heroes who can be safely imitated and admired.

See selections listed under Hero and Heroine Stories in Index of My BOOK HOUSE, Volume XII, page 247.

See also selections listed in Index, Volume XII, under:

Ambition-Leadership........p. 284   Faith-Reverence...........p. 287
Bravery-Courage...........p. 284   Overcoming Difficulties-
Cheerfulness-Friendliness ...p. 285   Perseverance-Resource-
Cooperation...............p. 286   fulness.................p. 288
Fair Play-Honesty.........p. 286   Patriotism...............p. 288

See Index of My BOOK HOUSE, Volume XII, Countries of the World, page 235, for stories about people of all nationalities which will create a feeling of friendliness and racial tolerance. See also selections listed under Tolerance, in Index, Volume XII, page 289.

My BOOK HOUSE supplies unusual reading material in the home which helps the child with assembly programs and other school activities.

My BOOK HOUSE includes selections which challenge the child's thinking and arouse his desire for the worthwhile; increase his scope of knowledge and help him feel adequate to meet real life situations. See selections listed under Biographical Sketches in Index, Volume XII, page 230.

IN YOUR HANDS

What the School Expects of Your Child
In Grades Seven, Eight and Nine—Continued

MUSIC

To sing for enjoyment and develop interest in glee club.
To develop an appreciation of music and to impart musical facts.
To learn about the great composers and their music.
To listen to compositions played by orchestras or on recordings.
To arrange programs for special occasions.
To arouse interest in playing instruments.

HOME-SCHOOL CHARTS

Where to Find Help in My BOOK HOUSE
For Grades Seven, Eight and Nine—Continued

See chapter XXIII of this book.

See selections listed under Music in Index of My BOOK HOUSE, Volume XII, page 254. Interesting stories and notes of over 60 composers from the 17th Century through the Modern Period are included.

Illustrations of musical instruments are listed in the Index of My BOOK HOUSE, Volume XII, page 257.

Suggested reading in My BOOK HOUSE for grades seven, eight and nine:
Volume V, page 222 (Note)
Volume VI, pages 58, 144, 159
Volume VII, page 72 (Note)
Volume VIII, pages 18, 188 (Note)
Volume IX, pages 98, 120 (Notes), 134 (Note), 151 (Notes)
Volume X, pages 11 (Note), 44, 89, 98 (Note), 119 (Note), 154 (Note), 165 (Note), 203 (Note)
Volume XI, page 73
Volume XII, pages 163, 168

Detailed instructions for making homemade musical instruments are given in the Packet of *Creative Work for Your Child's Hands.*

CHAPTER XVI

Climbing the Ladder of Years

By Martin L. Reymert, Ph. D.

Director, The Mooseheart Laboratory for Child Research

CLIMBING THE LADDER OF YEARS is a valuable year-by-year guide prepared especially for My BOOK HOUSE by Dr. Martin L. Reymert, an internationally-known child psychologist. It is presented in a series of articles covering the outstanding phases in your child's physical, mental, emotional, social and personality development from birth through early adolescence, and is based on scientific research and personal observation of thousands of children. My BOOK HOUSE Plan offers this series as a guide to help reveal to parents the reactions and development that may be expected of the normal child.

Help your child mature fully at each age level and set his standards in accordance with his mental maturity. Many children fail only because they are exposed to situations that they are unable to solve *at that particular time*. CLIMBING THE LADDER OF YEARS will keep you in close touch with the things to expect from your child as he grows and develops and help you set standards comparable to his readiness for learning. Avoid pushing him beyond his own level of understanding and you will enable him to experience the thrill of success and accomplishment rather than failure and discouragement.

In making use of these standards and steps of development, it should be borne in mind at all times that individual children differ from one another and may differ from these standards. Thoughtful parents, then, should not be over-anxious if their children do not conform exactly. When actually measured, each child has his own rate of development; his mental development may be at one level, his social development on another, and his physical on still another.

These standards then should be regarded as helpful approximations of normal development and should not be interpreted as rigid demands on any individual child.

THE LADDER OF YEARS

THE BUDDING OF LIFE:
YOUR CHILD'S FIRST YEAR

ERHAPS the greatest single finding of psychology and the biological sciences is that there are no two human beings alike. When a child is born we have a human being the exact like of which has never existed in the world's history and never will exist in the future. Being unique from the start, all the inborn abilities and talents of the child will be either enhanced or retarded by environmental conditions, and what we call "character and personality" will be mainly a product of what the infant comes in contact with during his first years of life. From the first day of life, conditions begin to mould him. From then on, we, as parents, must realize our tremendous responsibility and it might truly be said that there is no more difficult or important position in life than that of parenthood.

What we think of as "intelligence" has its earliest developmental roots in the first stages of the child's gaining control of his body, learning to react to people as social beings, such as recognizing familiar persons, giving different kinds of emotional reactions,—all these are signs of budding intelligence. In other words, *learning* in all directions and of all things starts at birth. While he can suck and swallow from the start, the child also soon learns to grope for the nipple, to turn his head towards it, and even later to seek it with his hands. Thus exploration and inquiry is already apparent. All his senses, through which he gains his knowledge, develop at a tremendously rapid rate in the first year. At first he gazes fixedly at the bright light, but in the second month he begins to follow moving objects with his eyes. At four weeks of age the infant begins to be definitely aware of different kinds of sounds and to show pleasure in his mother's handling him.

107

IN YOUR HANDS

Social reactions also show up early. At the age of a few weeks, the infant stops crying at the sound of his mother's voice which marks the first understanding of language. By the end of the first month, the child has a repertoire of sounds, coos, gurgles, whimpers, etc., which tell his mother that he is either content and happy or uncomfortable. Before there is any understanding of words or phrases, he will laugh and gurgle as answer to a playful frolicsome tone so from the start the mother should recognize the need for watching her voice in speech and later in reading aloud.

While actions such as those of eye and hand movement grow more complex and more coordinated, one of the fundamentals of intelligence—memory—begins to show itself increasingly during the second half of the first year. He smiles or laughs at the very sight of food; he laughs when his clothes are put on him to go out. He begins to perceive relationships. For instance, if he drops something he knows enough to look on the floor for it, if a block is out of reach he pulls the table cover to bring it to him. At the end of the first year, he begins to try to imitate the words and actions of others. He is especially fond of definite rhythmic sounds in either music or nursery rhymes. He is now quite a social being, uses sounds and perhaps single words to get attention, laughs and cries when others do, etc.

Thus, by the end of the first year, the child in a rudimentary way uses all the ingredients of intelligence and understanding, has developed, for him, characteristic habits of manipulation, of self-expression and of reaction to other human beings, which we may deem good or bad and which may stay with him throughout his life. By pampering and over-indulgence we might make him selfish and unfit for society or, by correct educational procedures, inculcate self-reliance and social-adaptability. At this time, we parents can make the child fond of a well-modulated voice in conversation and reading, lay a foundation for the aesthetic appreciation of color and form and make the start for the child's discerning of values.

YOUR CHILD'S SECOND YEAR OF LIFE: 12 TO 18 MONTHS

AT this time your child literally crosses the threshold of a new world. From his first few faltering steps, he learns to walk, conquering space. While the world before had to come to him, now he can go to it. By climbing he can reach hitherto unobtainable heights. He runs around for the sheer joy of running, opens drawers and cupboards, even takes books and turns the pages, perhaps two or three at a time. He is now as sincere an explorer as Admiral Byrd of his own "Little America," a world which, with Stevenson, "is so full of a number of things."

He now begins to get more definite experiences of success and failure which mould his character and personality into patterns which might last throughout life. Now we parents must be on the alert, thinking that this baby will some day be somebody's husband or wife, and will have to fit into some occupation or profession. His character and temperament will now be apparent and may be influenced in many ways. If he cannot open a drawer or if he climbs and falls, he may meet these situations with either a temper tantrum or a persistent try-and-try-again. So characteristic is his behavior already in this early stage that he is apt to be labeled, for instance, as "stubborn and persistent" or "placid and easy-going."

Now, too, he makes his first real use of language. While most of his words may still be incomprehensible to adults, he now uses his few words not as "tricks" but actually to communicate ideas. He learns to let his mother know that he wants to "eat," he wants "water," etc. He also tells the world how he feels. He no longer merely cries loudly to express his different emotions as pain, anger and fear but his face and voice now become a mirror to the mother which tells her more than a thousand words.

He is gaining in self-assurance and self-control. His memory span is now longer. He recalls where he put things, remembers what his mother does not want him to do, and relates one experience to the other. For instance, he pretends to read the paper or the book and he shows how daddy smokes his pipe. He expresses much of his understanding by imitation and is extremely interested in all things going on.

Whereas in the first year he was only beginning to recognize the form of things and to pay little attention to his own crayon scribblings on paper, now the pictures are no longer mere blotches to him but take on meaning. He points to the picture of the "kitty," a "boy," "house," or "car." Nursery rhymes, jingles, and simple musical themes enthrall him. The book is more than an object to hold, it has something in it to look at!

Now the parents, through their own play with the child, may greatly enhance or hinder the development of his rapid steps of learning. Let us remember that while the child gropes out violently for himself in this period, we parents should make the world in which he roams worthwhile and constantly stimulating to him. The child's day should be well-ordered. He should have definite play periods with his parents and family but should also learn to amuse himself while alone, having around him things stimulating to the various activities of which he is capable at this age.

There is definite danger here that loving mothers will be of too much assistance, give too much attention, in short, be over-solicitous. This, carried to the extreme, may give us the future "clinging-vine" woman or the man who will always have difficulty in standing on his own feet.

THE LADDER OF YEARS

YOUR CHILD'S SECOND YEAR OF LIFE: 18 TO 24 MONTHS

O N the basis of modern research, the second year of life is fundamental and critical in so many ways that books could be written about what parents should and should not do in this pliable period. As we now follow the tiny adventurer through his day, we find him walking upstairs without assistance, stopping with both feet on each step, still having great difficulty in making sudden stops or in changing his direction without losing his balance. He pulls off his socks himself, carries familiar objects from place to place, drinks from a cup and eats from a spoon, knows that an apple can be eaten but that a block cannot. He no longer just throws his blocks around but can build a simple tower.

He can point to parts of his body upon request. He has what the psychologists call quite an extensive "picture-vocabulary." If shown pictures of simple objects like a clock, scissors, basket, table, house, etc., he can name them. The child's world at this time can be greatly expanded by an intelligent and systematic use of interesting pictures suited to his interests and capacities. Since primitive man's scribblings on the rocks, pictures have always been a most valuable means of imparting information and knowledge. Even highly intelligent grown-ups, when words fail or are inadequate, take to the pencil for an explanatory sketch or drawing.

The child now likes to talk to himself or others, even when he obviously has nothing to say. He prattles with his newly-found words much as he formerly gurgled in his crib. At the end of the second year, the child has an average vocabulary of 300 words. Here, as throughout these articles, it should be remembered that normal children vary widely in their rate of development. Thus, a child with ten words at this time might in a few months spurt up his vocabulary tremendously. The words have unequal value, however, some being a little more than just sounds while others, even when used alone, might signify a full sentence. His words are mostly names of things, persons, actions and situations. He is beginning to use words such as "me," "my," "it," etc., showing that he identifies himself as distinct from others. There is no question but that wise stimulation by parents or members of the family in the line of combining appropriate pictures with words will greatly aid his growing vocabulary.

He is fond of rhythms and likes to hum and sing. The reading aloud of suitable nursery rhymes combined with well-executed pictures of persons, things and actions, is increasingly valuable as it all may be gradually grasped by the child. He now uses simple sentences, sing-songy in rhythm and sound patterns which mark the primitive stages of music and poetry. He now smiles in recognition when he hears the same nursery rhyme over and over again. Not only does the child profit by this repetition but he actually likes and appreciates it.

His emotional life is broadened, he shows spontaneous affection, signs of pity, sympathy, modesty and shame. He pouts when he is scolded, smiles when praised and shows evidences of guilt when he has broken a vase and may hang his head in disgrace. He is still very self-centered and rather content to be occupied all by himself. He is, however, becoming conscious of the family group, hiding his toys from the others, doing simple domestic tasks such as getting slippers for daddy, showing his toys and things to others. Much of this is pure imitation but some of it also expresses his reactions to definite situations and relationships.

Wide-awake parents should, at this time more than ever, realize that the tree will develop and grow according to the way in which the natural needs of the seedling are being met.

THE LADDER OF YEARS

YOUR CHILD'S THIRD YEAR

OVING around quite freely now, the child learns more and more to cope with his environment, trying to change it to suit himself and trying to understand it, continuously investigating and exploring. He is meeting up with natural events and nature, both in the home and on the outside. He notices plants growing, flowers spreading out in their diversity of color, the cat and doggy jumping, sleeping, eating, and behaving in various ways and possibly reproducing themselves. He experiences sickness and recovery in himself and others, he notices rain, thunder and lightning, snow and sunshine, the change of season, the heavenly bodies—the moon and the stars. He meets up with different temperaments in the family group and in his start in the nursery school, he tumbles up against new personalities of children a little older and a little younger than himself. Indeed, his is a complicated world!

Naturally, his curiosity grows in leaps and bounds and he is capable of questioning all around him, formulating small sentences and increasing his vocabulary to some one thousand words by the end of the third year, all of which, however, are not meaningful to him as yet. He is now building a definite vocabulary for *social* understanding and wants to "help" in everything that everybody in the family does. He likes to imitate people, the delivery boy, the candy-store man, the doctor, etc., and not so much out of a desire to act but rather because he likes to do something where he can use words—where he can talk. There are questions galore about everything and he asks the same ones over and over again, such as: "Why does it rain?" "Where does the sun go?" "What makes the car go?" "Do you love me?" etc., etc. Such questions

113

should be intelligently answered by parents each time since his repetition means that he is groping for knowledge and security. Naturally, many of the new experiences are also apt to evoke fears, some of which might indeed follow the child throughout life if we parents do not give proper explanations concerning what to fear and what not to fear.

While now he has learned to listen and listens to learn, stories can be depended upon to hold his interest and to keep him absorbed more than they did previously. He likes to hear the new words and to grasp meaning from them. He will retell stories, keeping the book before him as if he actually reads. He wants to hear the same story time and time again and will correct the reader if any changes in wording are introduced. The wisdom of the ages being embodied in nursery rhymes, simple fables, and folk tales, the child may have his world of ideas and experiences greatly expanded at this time by intelligent reading material and pictures.

In his personal habits he now can wash his hands unaided and button his coat. He walks the stairs one foot to each step, helps with household tasks and tries to "show off" in many ways. Emotionally he now definitely expresses jealousy, anger, and might have brief temper tantrums, often directed against an offensive toy or a chair in his way. He knows what he is allowed and what is forbidden. Now the foundations are laid for whether he or she will become a socially well-balanced personality.

We parents must be patient but firm with the talkative and constantly questioning child of three to four years, and be conscious of the fact that he must now be shown attention and affection by others, thus giving him a feeling of security. We must enhance his world by stories, pictures and new experiences inside and outside of the home. We should help him when he needs it but let him do what he can for himself so that he may develop self-assurance and self-reliance.

THE LADDER OF YEARS

YOUR CHILD'S FOURTH YEAR

WHEREAS at three your child was a little quaint and naive, a baby in the process of becoming a little boy or girl, now he is sophisticated in his ways. His amateur command of words and ideas makes him seem much older than he was just a short year before. His tendency to speak out, to assert himself with words may give us the impression that he knows actually more than he does.

He is now a better runner than he was. Instead of being able to jump only up and down as he could before, at four he can make a broad-jump, both running and standing. He can even skip in a kind of lame duck manner. He likes to try different kinds of stunts. He is also better at doing things that require fine coordination. He can button his clothes and lace his shoes very easily.

At four your child will be intellectually busy with many things but not profoundly absorbed with any one thing in particular. His language ability is increasing through the endless questions he asks. Since his speech still has sounds that are reminiscent of the baby, his eternal questioning and talking may be the means of giving him the necessary practice for improving his enunciation, making his speech smoother and less labored.

He doesn't like to repeat things but he can carry on rather long conversations and can even tell a lengthy story mixing up fact with fiction.

He comprehends very little of the past and the future, and lives mainly in the present. In stories he manifests a limited interest in the plot itself. When he listens to stories he tends to act out what is happening in a muscular sense, assuming the bodily

115

postures and gestures of the characters. Therefore, simple stories that have a great deal of physical action and not too much plot appeal strongly to him at this age.

At four his drawings will not be artistic or even reasonably complete from an adult point of view, but they do show that he is paying attention to some details. In drawing a man, he will draw perhaps a head, no body, but on the head will be two appendages that may be ears, or arms or legs. He may even include two eyes.

He will tend to be a little bit bossy to those children younger than himself, he will tend to make flat, dogmatic statements, to be reasonably self-reliant in his personal habits. He goes to the toilet by himself with very little help. He can dress and undress himself with some assistance, he combs his hair and brushes his teeth with a little guidance. He can even talk while eating without half choking himself.

In his play activity he tends to play *with* children rather than play *along side* children as he did earlier. He will share things brought from home in the group of three or four children with whom he prefers to play. When he does play by himself he often talks to an imaginary playmate. At this age it will be noted that he is very good at making up excuses and alibis. This alibiing shows that he is becoming conscious of a social world outside himself, of other people who have opinions and attitudes.

However, in spite of his growing reasoning powers, he does tend to have a great many unreasonable fears—fear of the dark, fear of some animal, fear of thunder and lightning.

He may also indulge in telling stories, pure fabrications, or *lies* by adult standards. These stories, however, just denote his growing imagination, and we parents must be careful in gradually and intelligently making him aware of the difference between fiction and reality. Because he is so young, he cannot distinguish at this time between truth and untruth. These stories of his will supply him with adequate social orientations if the parents handle the situation properly.

As parents we should be aware of our duties at this stage of a child's growth, of acquainting him pleasantly with the animal world and his physical surroundings in order also to eradicate fears. Getting stories of approved and classical value is a great help in this. Attendance in Nursery School is also of great value.

IN YOUR HANDS

YOUR CHILD'S FIFTH YEAR

YOUR child's fifth year marks the end of the period of early childhood. At this time he will appear to be quite adult-like in his mannerisms and general air of sophistication. He will no longer be tied so strictly to his mother's apron strings. He is more agile now. He skips and jumps well, he can even balance himself on his toes for several seconds or more. He keeps better time to music when he dances. At this time he is a ready pupil for dancing and physical exercises.

He is more self-dependent and self-sufficient than before and understands his world and his own place in it better. Now he will probably be in the kindergarten and should easily adjust himself to being away from home for a period of time.

In the home he will be rather more dependable and obedient. He doesn't dawdle as much in what he is doing. He may show an interest in sweeping, washing and wiping dishes. He may show a tendency to protect his younger playmates. In his speech he shows definite evidence of politeness and tact, another indication of increasing sociability.

Emotionally, he is not capable of complex emotions, any possible tragedy is not fully understood. However, in simple everyday circumstances he shows a variety of emotional characteristics and attitudes. He can be serious, patient, friendly, meticulous, satisfied, pleased at some accomplishment, etc.

He is now having personal friends. He plays with them in groups of from two to five. At the dinner table he is very sociable and talkative. There is less tendency to quarrel. He is much aware of competition, and exerts himself more when competing with others. In his speech, there should no longer be any sign of "baby" articulation providing the parents have not encouraged it.

118

THE LADDER OF YEARS

By this time he has mastered the grammatical intricacies of the language and expresses himself in complex sentences. His vocabulary has increased by fifty per cent since the age of four, mostly because of his new contacts in kindergarten and the neighborhood.

In answering questions he is briefer and more to the point than a year earlier. He is less inclined to ramble. When he asks questions he asks to find out the answers. He actually wants to know. His questions have immediate application to the world around him. He wants to know what things are for and what they do. An auto is to ride in, a book is to look at, a spoon is to eat with, a telephone is for talking to someone who is not there.

He pays a good deal of attention to details. Now he can draw a picture of a man that is recognizable. He can isolate the particular word or phrase in conversation that puzzles him rather than reacting to the statement as a whole.

His school and playmate experiences have taught him many socialized games. In his outdoor toys he prefers most his tricycle or his sled. He is interested in pasting and tracing pictures, he can string beads and cut out pictures with scissors and draw with crayons. In his drawing, he has a definite idea of what he wants to draw before he starts. Previously he would just draw and then decide what it was he had drawn.

His appreciation of time and the duration of events develops. In stories his interest turns to plot and sequence. He can retell a story, remembering the plot and the order of events. He will carry over his play activity from one day to the next and he shows a memory for remote events and places. Yesterday and tomorrow take on a definite meaning for him.

Now is the time for parents to realize that he has reached the stage in his development where interests, capacities, and activities make him ready to go into the outside world of the *neighborhood* and the *school*. Have we prepared him well for this rather sudden great expansion of his personal universe?

YOUR CHILD'S SIXTH YEAR

N the year from five to six, your child will again be entering upon a new phase of life. This is the time when he is prone to venture farther from home unaccompanied, and if he has been allowed to gradually explore the immediate neighborhood "on his own hook," he will generally have returned home safely and have gained confidence in orientation to a larger environment.

He should dress himself independently except for such difficult things as tying his shoe laces or tie. He should brush his own teeth, wash himself with a little supervision, keep his room and his own personal belongings in order. He should have the responsibility for such things as feeding the cat or dog, watering his own plants, putting away his wagon or bicycle when through playing. He should now have the first introduction to the uses of money and should be permitted to make small purchases such as a penny's worth of candy or a two-cent balloon. Through all these activities the child is developing attitudes of self-reliance, independence and orderliness.

Individual parents will know best which small daily duties to give their child at this time. It is a safe statement that if the child is not trained to definite duties in this period, parents may later find it very hard to inculcate in him the willingness to assume and fulfill responsibilities properly—a characteristic so necessary for adjustment in later life. Stories and fine examples on this topic of self-reliance and responsibility, as found in the literature of My BOOK HOUSE, will be of great help in this period.

At this time, too, the child tends to be less imitative of others and is becoming more of an individual. His personality characteristics are becoming more marked and typical of him. Children differ as widely in personality make-up as adults. Some are aggressive, others are shy, timid, etc. Parents should understand this phase and should do everything possible to help the child adjust favorably. The retiring child should be encouraged to participate in group activities, he should learn to "take it" and also to "dish it out." Otherwise, being shy or timid, he will tend to look to his family for protection from his more aggressive playmates and too much of such protection tends to fix a set of habits which may be carried into adult life and make the individual withdrawn and dependent upon others. Your child should now be allowed to invite his playmates to his home over night and in turn to visit homes of friends when invited.

This socialized play activity will be increasingly important now. Play activities not only will have a greater variety but a greater proportion will consist of group games, like hide-and-go-seek, tag, jumping rope, races, rough-and-tumble, etc. This form of activity and freedom makes children more noisy, of course, but it also makes them more self-reliant under competitive conditions.

Another characteristic change in play activities is that activities which had formerly occupied only a relatively short period of time now hold his attention much longer. Thus by six, the child will often play "Cowboys and Indians," or "Father and Mother" for several hours or even for several days, continuing from the point at which he and his playmates previously left off. The child now makes further progress in that he will be playing simple table games like cutouts or coloring pictures, or stringing beads and he can work very simple two or four-piece jigsaw puzzles. Along the more gross motor activities he will probably learn to use a sled, perhaps to skate and to use a wagon—all definitely skilled activities.

After his long active day in this period, it is necessary to do something to relax the child in preparation for his much needed rest. It has been found that one of the most satisfactory and oldest methods of doing this is the telling of stories. At this age the child is capable of sustaining interest in long stories; he seems to enjoy them so much that he is often fond of having a story repeated on consecutive nights. Unlike the younger child, he now seeks for *meaning* in stories and in pictures and he is no longer content with merely knowing the contents of a picture. For this purpose, My BOOK HOUSE is ideal. Since it has the stories indexed according to titles, morals, subject, country of origin, etc., it is possible to illustrate by story and example not only the answers to the many questions the child asks, but also such matters as proper conduct and morals, which are often so difficult to convey understandably to the child. Thus the evening reading period may well become a time *for getting to really know your child* and to guide his development in the moral and spiritual aspects.

Further, your child is now upon the verge of receiving formal education. The words that he has learned to use, the ideas and relationships that he has gained now become the foundation upon which this education may rest. The more the child's life has been enriched by well chosen stories and experiences, the more likely will he find things at school familiar. He will more readily be able to find solutions to his problems aided by the ideas he has learned in the past. Your child's progress in school, his ability to get along with his playmates, to gain from new experiences, etc., is the product and the fruitage of all your efforts with him during the preschool years.

THE LADDER OF YEARS

YOUR CHILD ON HIS SIXTH BIRTHDAY

NOW that we have followed your child to his sixth birthday, we view the momentous event of his entering formal schooling. At this time it becomes increasingly important that all parents should know the characteristics of their own particular child in all details as apart from any other child of the same age. In other words, this should be a definite time in the child's progress when the father and mother should sit down and think of the kind of discipline they have given their child, the friends he has had, the stories they have told him, and all the stimuli which they have brought to bear on his development up to this point. Have we parents been the example we would be proud to have our child imitate? This is the time when outside help is often needed in order to get the true picture of the child in addition to the information which we parents have been able to gather from our general observations.

Time and again children of nine and ten years are brought to my laboratory because they are not getting along well in school. After a thorough examination, we often find that the main difficulty is poor vision or impaired hearing. Recently a child of ten who was considered a "dunce" by both teachers and parents, when tested on the audiometer was found to have impaired hearing. Another example, a child of eleven was brought to us with a reading difficulty. Poor vision was found to be her trouble and she was immediately referred to the oculist. Until this time, it had never occurred to the parents that this girl might have poor eyesight. Many such school problems might have been avoided by a general check-up at six years of age.

If a good pediatrician, a medical child specialist, has not followed your child systematically, this is the time that your child

123

should by all means be brought to him for a general physical check-up. This examination should include an evaluation of bone development, the child's state of nutrition, his sensory apparatus (vision and hearing).

At this time the parents will want to know more about the specific mental ability of their child so as not to expect too much or too little from him. As is well known, there is no better way to make a child extremely unhappy and sometimes to force him into misbehavior than for we parents to expect more of him than he can give. On the other hand, if we do not expect enough of him, he may never want to exert himself to the limits of his potentialities and therefore become restless and unhappy. Take him to a competent consulting psychologist who will check up on not only his "general intelligence" but on his special talents, his abilities and disabilities, his strong points and his weak points, personality characteristics, etc. A comprehensive report at this time by a competent psychologist[1] should give not only valuable information to the parents but should contain recommendations and general suggestions for the proper handling of the child in school and home. We should again remember that children of any age differ enormously among themselves in almost any trait or characteristic.

The science and techniques of child development have at their disposal well-tried and tested research methods. I would like to remind parents, in reference to this proposed check-up at six years, that both the biological and social sciences seem to agree that the human individual has his characteristics determined in all essentials by this time. Thus modern science confirms the Jesuit Father's statement, "Give me a boy from birth until he is seven years of age, then take him away and do with him what you will but I guarantee he will remain a true Jesuit."

[1]*Please write to me for the address of your nearest competent psychologist.*

THE LADDER OF YEARS

YOUR CHILD'S SEVENTH, EIGHTH AND NINTH YEARS
Part I: Physical and Intellectual Growth

AFTER the child reaches his sixth birthday, his development is less well defined in terms of year-by-year growth. He is now in the "middle period" of childhood. The kinds of activities he favors are those which make use of large muscles, such as running, bicycling, swimming, skating, acrobatic stunts, wrestling, and jumping. However, he also attempts highly skilled activities for which he is not quite ready; these include such acts as making doll dresses, drawing, and the use of tools to make aeroplanes or boats. He is not ready to do these skilled acts because the finer muscle groups in his fingers are not yet fully coordinated for such use, hence his desires often outrun his actual performance. But as these attempts are part of the physical development, his trials should be encouraged. Many toy tools, sewing kits and the like, sold in stores, are put up for use at different ages; the seven or eight-year-old child will usually have a simpler kit than the ten or eleven-year-old. We parents should be careful to choose those games and tools which sufficiently challenge our child's abilities and yet permit him the necessary success in completing tasks.

We can now notice our child becoming less and less dependent upon us. In his behavior about the house he seems to have "grown up." At meals he is able to use a knife to spread butter or jam or to cut his meat rather skillfully. You can rely on his being able to tell the correct time within a quarter-hour. He bathes and goes to bed without assistance. In the light of this increasing independence we see our child breaking the proverbial apron string. In his intellectual growth there has been a shift to more abstract thinking.

125

IN YOUR HANDS

He is better able to understand words and our answers to his questions. During this period the child becomes able to detect general similarities and differences between objects known to him—such as a baseball and an orange, an aeroplane and a kite. When he is told a story or a joke, he can detect the absurd elements.

During this period he begins to read on his own initiative. With an increased facility in reading, the child finds greater and greater pleasure in reading. He develops an ability to grasp the more difficult sentence structures and at the same time seems to enjoy the involved expressions used. During this period it is important that informative stories be made available to the child. For example, the care and feeding of pets can be learned by reading animal stories,—geographical and sociological information can be learned by reading stories about other peoples and their customs in their respective countries. We parents, however, should take care that the child's reading is not restricted to informative reading or reading for amusement. His reading should be guided into channels where he can read for a *purpose*, learn to follow directions to build things, etc. Such careful selection has already been made in My BOOK HOUSE collection. As the child learns to get the most out of his reading, he unconsciously acquires good reading habits that will aid his progress in school. It is advisable that the child should have certain periods for reading and that such reading should take place under proper lighting conditions.

In this period we see our child seeking a place among his friends through both physical and intellectual effort. His degree of success determines his position in relation to his friends. Encouragement and careful background guidance for the child's many activities at this time will repay us. We should realize that the child should be permitted to have more freedom in his activity, that we should furnish good reading material, and on the whole, a rich environmental stimulation in order that he may "reach out" for himself.

THE LADDER OF YEARS

YOUR CHILD'S SEVENTH, EIGHTH AND NINTH YEARS

Part II: Development of Social Behavior

AS the child grows physically and mentally during the years seven to nine, he naturally also gains in social experience. His school and extended neighborhood contacts are now giving him a much larger group of friends than he has had before his seventh year. Social participation on the playground, in school and in the neighborhood is characteristic of this period. However, there is a good deal of difference among children in their social tendencies and interests. Some of them will naturally be outgoing and happy, others will appear to be self-centered and prefer to be left alone. Some conditions which may influence a child's withdrawal to solitary play are: he might be aware that he is not like the other children physically, he may be too fat, too thin and skinny, extremely tall or short, he may wear thick glasses, he might be bow-legged or knock-kneed to extreme, or crippled in some manner. If the parents have not rationalized such conditions for him early in his life, the child may have no way of compensating for these defects. Just such a seemingly small matter as manner of dress may be of greatest importance. A child may be called a sissy when a mother insists on dressing him conspicuously different from others. Another child may not want to join the crowd because he is sensitive about his poor clothing. Even living in a home somewhat poorer than his friends might cause him to stay away from his more fortunate playmates. The brighter a child is, or the more retarded, or the more his background differs from the general run of the group, the more difficulties will he encounter; hence,

127

we parents need to exercise much understanding and patience.

Our child, during his seventh to ninth years of life, spends much of his time in play. Among his friends he likes to show off, he performs acts of daring, of speed, of skill. He tends to boast about his exploits and in order to add to his prestige he will often include the "great deeds" of his father or older brother. In turn, there is a brutal frankness in his judging the achievements and short-comings of his playmates and those of older persons. When he is with adults, he wishes to be treated as an adult and will often resent being called "my little man." His conversation with adults sometimes is annoying because of his curiosity and talkativeness. This is most true when he is prying into personal affairs or monopolizes the conversation of adults. We parents must bear with the experimenting growing child. We can suggest other activities to him and thus frequently prevent these annoyances, but to simply suppress natural behavior may lead the child to withdraw within himself entirely. Unsatisfactory response from parents to his social efforts may result in his going to others to seek the information, attention and approval which he craves.

The pleasure he derives from the company of others and the opportunities it gives him to perform before an audience makes him an active participant in the social events of the school, church, neighborhood and community. These events may be dramatic plays, picnics, celebrations, special field days, etc. Imaginative and dramatic play is very popular. Much time is spent in playing "house" and "cowboys and Indians."

Our child now goes to the movies on Saturday and also spends much time with the radio and newspaper. In many ways these media of entertainment are educational, even though so very much of what they offer is certainly not suitable for consumption by the young developing, sensitive mind and is apt to give the child a distorted picture of life. Fortunately, the young child misses most of the sordid meanings so readily grasped by the average adult audience.

Because we live in a world where it is important to know right from wrong, we spend a great deal of time trying to teach our child the difference. He, however, tends to behave in a manner that will give him the most satisfaction, regardless of whether it is right or wrong. Careful, but not too obvious guidance and consistent behavior by parents will gradually teach the child the "rules of the game" and of society. The kind of friends the child has outside of the home is also of great importance during this age period. In My BOOK HOUSE collection, many stories may be found that illustrate the accepted mode of behavior in various situations. Through such stories rules for proper conduct are easily transmitted to the child in a pleasing way.

A well-known student of child behavior has said that by nine years of age a child will be able to criticize his own actions and attitudes in an objective way. We should remember that although our subject is a nine-year-old child, he can think and he has a keen sense of justice regarding punishment meted out to him. We adults and parents should realize that the child is not willing to change a satisfying act merely because we say "don't." It is our business to suggest alternative constructive behavior. A child does not like to humiliate himself by acknowledging that he should not have taken Betty's doll, or taken the money that was lying on the table, but if we give him understandable explanations, he will gradually try to make up for his "misdeeds" by being good and not doing the destructive act again.

Social behavior is learned from experience only. There is, in spite of all modern devices in child care and training, no substitute for the good examples of parents.

IN YOUR HANDS

YOUR CHILD'S YEARS
NINE THROUGH TWELVE

Part I: Physical and Intellectual Growth

THE years from nine to twelve mark a stage in your child's development midway between late childhood and early adolescence. Physically, educationally and socially your child is changing. His abilities, activities, attitudes and interests reflect these changes. Physically the child is approaching the last stage of childhood and growth during this time will gradually begin to take on particular sex characteristics. In the period before puberty, the child should be prepared for the changes which are to take place. When the child first asked questions, showing an interest in sex and procreation, we parents should have answered his questions and explained any points about which he was in doubt. Such answers should be suited to the stage of development and understanding of the child at all times. The BOOK HOUSE FOR CHILDREN publishes separately the best little book now on the market, *How Life Begins*, which explains in story form all the salient aspects of "where babies come from" and intimately ties this up with procreation in the rest of the biological scale. The discussion of sex should always treat the subject as a natural biological phenomenon. Above all, a secretive, emotional, shamefaced or "nice-people-don't-talk-about-such-things" approach should be avoided since from this may ensue needless fears and inhibitions that prevent the child's best possible adjustment to life. Thus, the child will be prepared for the physical changes that come with adolescence and girls, especially, will be spared a great deal of needless anxiety with regard to the menstrual process.

130

THE LADDER OF YEARS

Along with physical development, physical prowess and manual dexterity increase during this period. The child is interested in and can do stunts and various kinds of acrobatics. He develops a degree of manual dexterity which satisfactorily enables him to carry out a wide variety of skilled acts. Conspicuously absent is the bungling uncertain trial-and-error manipulation of early childhood. Your boy in this period is reasonably efficient in the use of tools and especially quite handy with a pocket knife. He is interested in things which "work" or "run" and will construct these with either simple tools or by using the material of mechanical sets from which a variety of more or less "complicated machines" can be constructed. Expensive toy material is not necessary, though; he is just as thrilled about building a shack out of old boards and packing cases as he would be in having expensive lumber at hand. Your girl may make doll dresses of a rather complicated pattern; she will probably take a great deal of interest and show considerable skill in decorating her room. She will become increasingly skilled in performing household tasks and helping around the house.

In play interests and activities, competitive and cooperative play become more and more prominent. The games and sports become more complex and highly organized in response to the child's increasing bodily and manual skill. Further, the child is now at a stage where he can not only work with greater and more continuous effort but also have greater foresight and perseverance in achieving his goal. During this period your child will probably manifest an intense interest in such outdoor activities as hiking, swimming, skating, etc. Such activities as picnics, outings, hikes, etc., will have a great appeal. Indoors, table and card games are popular and engage a considerable portion of the child's playing time. Puzzles, problems, and tricks are also of great interest. Nowadays, a great deal of the child's time indoors is spent listen-

131

ing to the radio. There are special children's programs in the early evening hours, many of them not so good. At the present time just one such program is supervised by a child psychologist. We parents have a very difficult time controlling what our child shall listen to and what not. We should exercise our control of what should be allowed to go into the radio *at the other end* by sending in resolutions of protest, using P. T. A.'s and similar associations as public opinion "pressure groups."

Movies, too, offer a great appeal to this age group and the ideal selection is again difficult. Fears and nightmares from radio and movies can be greatly reduced if one of the parents will give full explanation to the child after each performance.

The outstanding avenue of intellectual development for this period is still the literature of the printed page. In school your child's reading skill has been increasing and with it his interest in reading. His reading preferences therefore undergo a similar maturation change. Instead of the simple stories and folk tales, your child will now prefer stories of adventure, stories of history, of famous people and events, of nature, of travel and faraway places. The outstanding selection of the world's best literature to be found in My BOOK HOUSE is particularly good in this respect. In the early part of this period you may be able to teach your child to use an encyclopedia, a dictionary or other book of reference in order to find information on what he is spontaneously curious about. By the middle of this period, his *reading vocabulary* (the words he can recognize and whose meaning he knows when he sees them in print) will exceed his speaking vocabulary (the words he uses in actual conversation). From this time on, progress in the knowledge of the meaning of words will come for the most part through books and literature. Boys especially prefer books or stories on adventure and athletics and enjoy articles on things to make and how to make them. Girls, on the other hand, not only enjoy similar books written especially for girls but are also equally interested in boys' books. Good reading habits can be fostered and built upon this natural interest of the child. There is an old saying, "Tell me your friends and I'll tell you what you are!" It is equally true that if you "tell me the books you read, I'll tell you what you are!"

IN YOUR HANDS

YOUR CHILD'S YEARS 9 to 12

Part II: The Development of Social Behavior

DURING the period of nine through twelve years of age the outstanding line of developmental progress is not so much in physical or intellectual behavior as in what might be called social behavior. It is in this field that the most well-defined and noticeable changes are taking place.

Parents will notice a distinct change in the kind of activities in which the child participates. The sports he or she engages in now will put a higher premium on *team play* as opposed to individual play. Development in skilled performance will be along the lines of the kind of specialization which team play requires. More than mere specialization and skill, however, is involved here. In team play the individual is subordinated to the team somewhat, and the child will experience some degree of conflict between his desire for individual recognition and superiority and his desire for the success of the team. Such team play will furnish the best kind of training in cooperation and sportsmanship for later life.

Another rather significant characteristic of this period is the formation of formal group organizations, gangs and clubs with a limited membership and with various secret rituals, rites, signs, handclasps, etc. The clubs are usually made up of children of similar ages and the same sex. Through them the child identifies himself with his group. Besides socializing the child and making him observant of the rules of the group, such clubs furnish an outlet for his creative social talents and organizing and cooperative abilities. These clubs taking their cues from the organizations of grown-ups may stage a show or small carnival or lemonade sale to raise funds. They have their dues, their meetings, their officers and their rules. They represent a feature in the child's social behavior distinct and different from anything in his earlier life.

However, club organization does not cut across sex lines because at this stage the boys feel awkward, shy and ill at ease in the presence of girls, and girls are likewise discomfited, though less so, in the presence of boys. Here we have the first indication of the social differentiation between the sexes which definitely heralds pre-adolescence.

Hero-worship manifests itself during this period. In most instances the hero is an actual person whom the child admires and tries to imitate rather than a fictional character. It may be a movie star or a neighborhood "big shot" or an admired relative. Though the child's ideals and aspirations are rather transitory during this time and follow one another in rapid succession as the child changes heroes, parents should nevertheless realize the importance of this hero-worship in affecting the outlook and behavior of the child and should consciously strive to use this characteristic to mould the child's character and personality.

Pets are popular with both boys and girls. So marked is the interest in these that not only are the usual household dog or cat included but where there is the opportunity and circumstances permit, even a lizard or a mouse or pigeon may be some child's pet. The child also collects things during this period and often amasses quite a conglomeration. The objects collected may be stamps, gum wrappers, pictures of movie stars or baseball players, tinfoil, pins, buttons, coupons, match covers, etc. Interest in collections is almost continuous during this time though the kinds of things collected may vary with the circumstances and changing interests. A last important feature of this period is the manifestation of an increasing self-reliance and dependability in the child. With his new capacities comes a certain urge to independence and initiative. Some children find ways of earning money for themselves by doing odd jobs for neighbors, carrying groceries or delivering papers after school. The child can now be trusted to go about his home town freely. He will make minor purchases for himself. At this time he writes occasional short letters to a vacationing friend, or a relative or a teacher. He answers ads and makes purchases by mail for booklets, samples, toys, gadgets, etc. He makes his own telephone calls, and in general is reasonably adept at the social use of this instrument. He can be trusted during the latter part of this period with taking care not only of himself but also of younger brothers or sisters.

There is a desire to be responsible for his own conduct and to make certain decisions and plans for himself. This increase in self-assertiveness on the part of the child is the first sign of the "declaration of independence" that typically comes with adolescence. Unless parents realize the significance of this, unless they know and are prepared to use this tendency to help the child stand on his own feet, a great deal of conflict and misunderstanding may occur. One of the difficulties is that sometimes the child's capacities compel us to treat him like an adult and at other times his immaturity and lack of experience make an outside authority necessary. This inconsistency of treatment works hardships on both parent and child. All this must be known and taken into consideration. It is definitely a phase in the process of the child's growing up and this should be given definite consideration in the program of "psychologically weaning" the child so that he will mature emotionally stable and independent.

TWELVE TO FOURTEEN
THE EARLY ADOLESCENT PERIOD

IN our twelve-year-old we parents will now be able to see in bold relief the results of what we have or have not done in furnishing the right environment and training for our boy and girl from the first day of life. In all respects the main foundations were laid in the preschool period and everything that has since happened to our child has left a trace. The years from twelve to fourteen foreshadow the radical changes of adolescence—changes in body and mind, in interests, activities and attitudes. The young boy or girl begins to change into the young man or young lady. This period and the following two years are utterly different from those that have gone before in that development now does not show as rigid and as well-defined patterns. Now the changes that are taking place in children of the same age vary greatly. Tall Johnny Jones at thirteen may have acquired a deep voice and even a bit of peach fuzz on his cheek which he is trying to cultivate, train and coax into becoming sideburns, while his friend, Bill, who is of exactly the same age, may still have a peaches and cream complexion, a high-pitched young boy's voice and be a couple inches shorter than Johnny. This fact of the widely differing rates of growth in different individuals in this period should be greatly stressed so that we parents do not feel that our Johnny is either growing up too fast or too slow or that our Mary has grown up too quickly and is no longer a little girl. The body has its own internal mechanism of growth regulation, different for different individuals, normal for any one case. In this period the girl usually enters her puberty, the time of differentiation when the body changes to assume adult characteristics, pubic hair, wider hips, budding breasts, etc. The boy's puberty comes later. With this change in body form, Mary will no longer be getting her clothes in the girls' section but will have graduated to the "young miss department" and her outfit must conform to the peculiar prevalent fads of her group (saddle shoes, "sloppy joe" sweaters, etc.).

With this greater physical maturity bestowed by nature, Mary's own conception of herself will change. Parallel with her dropping her former childish pre-occupations, activities and amusement (for instance, playing with a doll is strictly "passé"), is her assuming an adult air, a pseudo adult outlook and a conception of herself as "grown up." Younger children in the family or neighborhood, the "small fry," are the first to feel and notice this change since it manifests itself in an ill-concealed attitude of condescension toward them, the definite implication that they are somehow lesser beings by virtue of her exalted status. We, as adults, will notice it too and, of course, it will seem entirely out of character and definitely exaggerated. However, we should not laugh, poke fun or jibe at these symptoms of growing up. This is a period of change and readjustment and we parents by our treatment of and attitude toward the child can do a great deal to facilitate the readjustment.

With girl friends her own age, Mary is forming a social group which is different from the rather spontaneous playgroups of an earlier period in that membership rather than being casual is conscious and active. There are certain standards for "belonging"; certain standards of dress and conduct are demanded. One or two girls in the group may be Mary's especial friends, her chums, and in these smaller more intimate units close confidences are exchanged.

Toward girls older than she, Mary looks for examples or models in dress, bearing, general air, mannerisms, conduct and behavior.

138

Hence, the importance of Mary's having the right kind of older girl companions. She and her group are interested in the adult world very much at this time, not the world of old fogeys (i.e., anyone over twenty-one years or so), but older adolescents— exalted beings like juniors or seniors in high school. Parents are apt to be chagrined at having their authority refuted by a quotation of the opinion of some older adolescent who is by some mysterious process presumed to have knowledge, experience and wisdom far beyond that of parents and older people. However, we should realize that this is natural, that it represents an evidence of "psychological weaning." It indicates a feeling of sufficient difference of point of view and outlook on the part of the child to make *our* information seem inapplicable to her problem or question.

During this period Mary will begin to look at boys a little bit differently. Seen through her eyes they are undergoing subtle but none-the-less important changes. No longer will they be merely playmates. They become of interest for their own sake, as boys, as examples of the opposite sex toward whom girls are beginning to act differently than they do toward girl companions. Their mixed play, instead of being directed by absorption in the game itself, characteristic of earlier periods, now is merely a vehicle or means for mutual association. Thus in games of tag there is a tendency for boys to chase girls and vice versa, rather than random or indiscriminate tagging. Lulls in activity are similarly lacking in spontaneity and are self-conscious. There is a lot of just standing around, at a distance, talking, teasing, even arguing, with jibes and name-calling. The social graces and the smooth talk is a thing of the future and the children now just grope about for something to be doing or saying, often something that covers up their lack of sophistication of experience, insecurity and lack of self-confidence.

While Mary undergoes rather marked changes during these two

years, Johnny undergoes relatively slight changes. Boys, in general, mature a little later than girls. Hence, Johnny is not too radically different from what he was a little earlier. In these two years his development is extended along previously indicated lines. He is largely interested still in his group activities whether they be his gang, his particular secret society, athletic club, baseball or football team. Being a little older now he can more freely engage in the activities in which he has been interested all along, the "man stuff" activities such as fishing, camping and hunting. We parents have all too likely grown accustomed to thinking of him as "our little Johnny" and this attitude should be shed in favor of one which recognizes his greater skill, ability and maturity and grant him the greater freedom that his widened scope of activities and interests necessitates. This is the time for individual hobbies and in these we should let the child's own interests be the guide. All along, the "apron string" should grow less binding. The Boy Scouts have special appeal at this time as well as other similar organizations which take the boy outdoors. Here are provided not only the group spirit and solidarity as exemplified in pledges, laws, secret signs, ritual, etc., but also the organization of activity in which the child can exercise his skill and abilities not only in competition with other individuals but also in competition with his own past record.

In this period Johnny will begin to get the first faint glimmerings of the desirability of a clean face and finger-nails and combed hair, and the contrast in his attitude will bring relief to parents. In these matters, as the French say: "Look for the woman!" Johnny is becoming interested in girls, perhaps even a special one. Of course, he does not have the "line" or the confident manner to single her out but, rather, he may tease her more than the other girls or manage to be near her to hold her hand in games rather oftener than mere chance could provide. These are the first vague manifestations of "puppy love" considered by psychologists both necessary and very important as a basis for the later selection of the real mate.

In social gatherings, parties, entertainments, church socials, etc., the children get their first opportunity to meet each other on a more formal footing, a preview of what high school life will be like. These contacts are attended by a great deal of self-conscious giggling on the part of both boys and girls, the girls may even in their naiveté be the aggressors. To begin with, they may stick to little clusters of self-conscious young folk, hoping to get from this small group contact a confidence and feeling of ease that they do not have individually. In all their social contacts the children are trying to acclimate themselves to a new situation in which there are new distinctions and in which new modes of behavior are expected of them. Naturally this requires a rather complete and thorough-going readjustment.

Indicative of this readjustment is the changed attitude in both boys and girls toward the world outside themselves. Whereas before the larger "outside" was mere convenient background for their activities, now it becomes increasingly a *social* world. The boy and the girl become aware of rules and regulations guiding conduct in society and become concerned with what other people think of them. On the verge of seeking admission to grown-up society, they have more regard for standards, tend to self-analysis, self-criticism and, surprisingly enough, to self-improvement. It is my opinion, for instance, that most of the customers for personality courses by mail, how to hypnotize, "be dynamic," how to build the body-beautiful, etc., exist in the adolescent group.

With this awareness of what the outside world thinks of them comes a more clear delineation in their own mind of themselves as individual personalities. Johnny will want to be considered "Johnny Jones" rather than accepting the anonymity of being

"Mr. Jones' son." They will want their own opinions and desires respected and given consideration rather than submitting unquestioningly and meekly to parental "say-so." Rather than trying to repress this tendency, we parents should recognize it as an important phase of growing up or of psychological weaning. We should make allowances and concessions to it in our discipline and way of thinking. Otherwise, we may either stifle this growing independence in the child or else have it express itself in behavior difficulties and open rebellion later on. While at this period we shall have to expect and understand a good deal of "day dreaming" through which the child is trying to understand himself and the world about him, we should also see to it that he continues to have definite routine duties within the family group.

The conception of the integrity of the individual is shown in the child's desire for privacy, for a certain little corner of the house, whether it be only a bureau drawer or an entire room, which is entirely his own, to which no other member of the family has access. Hence, Johnny and Mary will be asking for a key to their bureau, or to their trunk or whatever special place they choose for the repository of their most personal effects such as the much treasured diary. When this stage is reached, rather than be arbitrary, rather than assume the child is getting a little bit too independent, we should accede to this reasonable request. The things they wish to keep from us at this time most likely (if you remember your own childhood) are the things at which adults would smile if not laugh outright. The feeling of having some rights to privacy is not only a privilege but a necessity for the growing child at this age. Besides, we parents should be getting accustomed at this early date to the idea that certain affairs of our children are none of our business. Otherwise, we will cling to the much abused dominant attitude to the point where we may want

THE LADDER OF YEARS

to select the husband or wife for our child and even determine where and how his or her family shall live.

Indicative of this change in viewpoint of the youngster at this age is the way in which he spends his allowance. The girl may try to corner the market on beauty preparations, invade the dime store and return resplendent with rouge, lipstick, fingernail polish, eyebrow pencil, etc. The greatest amount of restraint is necessary on the part of the parent who first gazes upon his own sweet daughter beaming at him in full expectation of approval from under her camouflage of make-up. These initial jobs are characterized by liberal application rather than good taste. However, we must remember that while your daughter looks to you like a pagan voodoo medicine doctor in her war paint, in her own mirror she sees the blossoming likeness of Cleopatra, Helen of Troy, Scheherazade and other beauties of history. Guidance rather than repression of this tendency is the keynote in this situation.

Your young boy, rather than spending his money conservatively on school needs and candy throughout the week, may suddenly and unaccountably even to himself, under the bewitching influence of a certain pair of eyes, sink his entire allowance in two super deluxe hot fudge butter pecan ice cream sundaes topped with marshmallow whip and be impoverished for the rest of the week. We must take such points into consideration when a special session of the family financial committee is called to advance Johnny enough money for carfare to school for the rest of the week. Of course, such unwise spending should not be encouraged but special circumstances do arise in even the most well-ordered lives.

Representative, too, of the child's changing outlook are his reading interests which become more diversified. The familiar, the commonplace, the near-at-hand, are no longer interesting. Books now are expected to take the child out of his immediate world (the one he knows by experience), to introduce him to what he

143

IN YOUR HANDS

has not seen or known personally and to increase his scope of knowledge. Dramatized history, autobiography, travel and accounts of scientific discovery have a great appeal. However, in all of these there must be sufficient action and adventure to grip the interest of the reader. Adventure and action stories *per se* have their large group of adherents and quality varies from Huck Finn to the dime novel thriller. In the field of literary and reading interests we will now be able to harvest the results of our guidance of the boy or girl in their earlier years. If we succeed in laying the right foundation, we will have a child with an alert, active mind, responsive to a wide scope of cultural influences.

CHAPTER XVII

Creative Expression in Children

G REAT creative energy exists in every normal child and he is continually searching for ways to express this energy in words and action. It is true that few children may be potential artists when we think of artists only as exhibitors of fine paintings, sculptors or accomplished musicians. But, on the other hand, *all* children for the sake of their own well-rounded emotional development need many opportunities to express their ideas, feelings and emotions by handling and experimenting with materials.

The child who is able to make the dreams of his imagination come true by modeling in clay, writing a story or poem, building a model airplane, etc., will be inspired to work out his ideas again and again. Everything the child creates, no matter how crude, serves to give him confidence in his own ability.

Let Him Experiment With Materials. The child does much of his thinking through handling materials and making them express his ideas. It is the parent's responsibility, then, to see that the child is free to express himself in a creative way during his early years at home. Clay, paper, chalk, crayons, paint, wood, blocks, sand, cloth and finger paint, are but a few of the materials children can use to express their ideas in a creative manner. Something creative can be made from every material, but you may find that some will have a stronger appeal to your child than others. Your child may hesitate or even fail in his efforts to express his ideas with chalk or crayons only to discover clay or paint an excellent medium. It is best, then, to encourage him to try his hand at many different materials in order that he may choose the ones he prefers. Let the child decide on the materials that will best express his own ideas. Show him the mere fundamentals of handling clay, give him the right size crayon and paper, and leave him to use these in his own way. Begin early to give your child a background of experiences and stories that will enrich his thinking and fire his imagination and the urge to create will follow naturally. The child should be allowed to create what he chooses—what he sees in his mind's eye— rather than encouraged to depend on others for ideas and directions. If he learns to use clay, paint or wood only in accordance with your definite instructions he will gain in his ability to handle the materials, but lose the opportunity to express himself in a creative way. The child's own crude creations will give him more satisfaction than the finest objects made by others.

Your Attitude Is Important. Do not place too much emphasis on the finished object your child has made. Be more concerned with the growth and understanding that has taken place within him while he was modeling his clay hen or drawing his version of the airplane he saw in the sky. The attitude you assume toward your child's work will influence his further attempts at creative expression. Be *enthusiastic* in your praise of the things he has done well and *casual* in your criticism and suggestions. Encourage him to finish the job he has started before he begins another; to persevere until he has learned to do the thing he started out to accomplish. Make him feel that you are anxious to help him in times of difficulty and praise his efforts that represent honest work. A simple suggestion about how to wipe the excess paint off his brush on the side of the paint jar may be the means of helping him overcome "runs" that are spoiling his pictures. Be sure to encourage the child's

CREATIVE EXPRESSION

original ideas and, at the same time, discourage thoughtless imitation. Anything that your child creates as a result of an inner experience is far more worthy of your praise than the cleverest copy of the work of others.

Ask Him to Tell You. It is better to ask the child if he would like to tell you about the interesting things he is doing than to ask, "What is it?" If your child feels that you do not understand what he is trying to do, he may think he has failed to do a good job. Very often his finished product will not reveal his original ideas to you. Little children let their imagination fill in the details that they are unable to work out with their hands and so it is usually best to let the little child tell you about his pictures in order that you may follow his thinking and better understand his efforts.

Child's Creative Work Is a Valuable Key to His Thinking. By carefully studying the details of your child's work you will have a valuable key to his thoughts and interests. You will be better able to interpret his emotional reaction to situations in the home and to new contacts at school and in the community. The objects your child creates will represent his sincere efforts to portray his impressions and record how well he has observed the important details of the things he has experienced. After a trip to the zoo, the child of *two* years will be satisfied to let a few strokes of the paint brush represent *his* idea of the roar of the lion. Sound and action appeal to him at this age and so he remembers them rather than the lion's form. The child of *three* may attempt to paint *his* impression of the same lion by blotches of paint on the paper; while the child of *four*, *five* or *six*, may record the mane of the lion as *his* most outstanding impression. The *six-year-old* may put his picture of a lion in a cage to show *his* sense of precaution or add other details that reflect his maturity of thought.

Unfoldment Recorded. As children grow and develop their creative work should record their maturity of thought and feeling. The older child's picture should show that he is observing important details and characteristics of the objects he is creating. If the impressions your child creates are stinted and lacking in understanding, it will indicate that he has not had enough experiences to clarify his thinking. His background will need to be constantly enriched with pictures, stories and firsthand experiences that will further his understanding and growth. The child's standard of perfection will grow *only* if the parent takes the time to let him *feel the need* for improvement.

The parent plays a most important role in encouraging and developing creative ability in the child. The parent's attitude toward his own daily work will tend to set the child's attitude for his own activities and chores. The more familiar the parent is with the things that make up the child's world, the more intelligent and sympathetic will be the guidance he is able to offer. Be tolerant and understanding in your attitude toward your child's work and you will find him exhibiting this same attitude in his criticism of the work of others.

Help your child feel the joy of accomplishment that comes from work well done and you will help him develop a lasting, happy, enthusiastic attitude toward work.

See Creative Expression on charts on pages 82 and 88 of this book and Creative Activities in Index of My BOOK HOUSE, Volume XII, page 283.

CHAPTER XVIII

Clay Modeling

CLAY is a splendid medium to stimulate imagination, observation and creativity in your child. It is so pliable that he can easily convert it into creative objects that represent his own ideas. You will find that your child will be able to translate his impression and feeling for form and proportion more realistically with clay than with other materials. Handling clay will give the child another outlet for his emotions and, at the same time, help him solve many problems of expression.

Clay may be purchased very inexpensively in five-pound containers at any department, school or art supply store. It comes in both moist and dry form. Dry clay flour is perhaps the most economical way to buy clay for home use as it may be mixed as you need it.

To make clay from clay flour, simply add two parts clay to one part water and mix and knead the mixture until it is about the consistency of putty. If you live in a section of the country where clay soil is available, you may mix this clay as you would the clay flour.

Plasticine is another modeling material that can be used over and over again as it does not harden.

Homemade Clay. If it is inconvenient to buy clay in your neighborhood, you may want to try this recipe for homemade clay:

MATERIALS:

1 cup of flour	1 cup of water
1 cup of salt	vegetable dye (optional)

Mix the ingredients thoroughly, with or without the vegetable dye. The dye is harmless but often makes the composition more attractive to the child. Heat the mixture slowly, stirring constantly, until it cooks away from the sides of the pan. Remove from the fire. It will be just lukewarm. Knead it with your hands until it has a claylike consistency.

Care of Clay. It is important that the clay you give your child is in good working condition so he can handle it easily without getting discouraged. The older child will want to mix his own clay and be responsible for keeping it in good condition. To keep homemade clay in modeling condition, put it in the ice box when it is not being used. It is a good idea to wrap the clay in wax paper and keep it in a covered glass jar. If homemade clay is left out

CLAY MODELING

of the icebox, it will dry out overnight. To keep commercial clay in modeling condition, it is necessary to wrap it in a damp cloth and place it in a covered can or jar when not in use. Hardened pieces of clay may be used over again by wetting them and kneading them into the right consistency.

Suggested Equipment for Clay Modeling. Clay is rather messy to use so it is advisable to let your child work with it in a place that can be easily cleaned. If he is working indoors, put a newspaper on the floor under his chair and table to catch the little crumbs of clay that fall. A few pieces of equipment will help the child get more satisfaction out of his experiences with clay. The following items are suggested for the home:

>Oilcloth cover for the table.
>Work board or piece of oilcloth on which to model clay (a discarded bread board is very satisfactory).
>Smock or coverall to protect his clothing.
>Small bowl or cup to hold water.
>Dull knife or smooth piece of wood to use for scraping and cutting clay.
>Covered jar or can to store clay when not in use.

A Child of Two Enjoys Playing With Clay. Even the child of two will enjoy experimenting with clay. At first he may object to the feel of it and dislike getting his hands dirty, but, after a few trials, he will come to enjoy it immensely. Place a lump of clay about the size of an orange on his clay board and he will begin patting and pounding it with the palms of his hands. He will squeeze it and roll it many times in order to

get the feel of it. He will try his hand at cakes and pies, or roll it in balls and coils. His piece of clay will take many forms in the course of five minutes and you will notice his expression of complete satisfaction as he quickly changes it from one crude form to another. Perhaps the shape of his clay will remind him of some object and he will want to tell you all about it. Working with clay gives the child many ideas and stimulates his desire to talk.

Let the Child Experiment. Children need many opportunities to manipulate the clay itself before they are ready to make objects and figures that we can recognize as such. The development of this skill of manipulation is rather a slow process in the child and depends largely on his muscular co-ordination and the opportunities he has had to handle the material itself.

At first, a round ball of clay may represent a fine horse or bunny to the little child. By the time he is *four*, he will begin to add details that will make his objects more authentic. The child's finished clay object will record his impression of the thing he is creating. The little child's attention span is brief and his muscles tire easily, so do not insist on his working with the clay when you see signs of fatigue.

If your attitude toward his work is a sympathetic one, the child will be encouraged to tell you many interesting details about it that you, no doubt, would overlook. Modeling in clay gives the child opportunities to work out many of his own problems.

A trip to see the real horse or bunny he has been trying to model, a chance to examine pictures in well illustrated stories, will often help direct the child's attention to the details he has omitted in his own creation. He will be more conscious of the form of the bunny, as he sees him hopping along, and more observant of his peculiar characteristics, when he hears the story describe the bunny's long, floppy ears and funny little cottontail. The same details he hears described so colorfully in his story will help awaken

CLAY MODELING

his own powers of observation and enable him to interpret his ideas more specifically.

Clay Is a Natural Medium for Children. Clay is a natural medium for the child to illustrate his favorite story characters. He will relive all the adventures of the *Gingerbread Man*[1], *Li'l' Hannibal*[2] or the *Little Engine That Could*[3], as he models these story friends in clay. He will enjoy saying his favorite nursery rhymes as he makes his clay take the form of Little Jack Horner[4] and his pie, or Humpty Dumpty[5] who sat on a wall. He will really be putting the words of his favorite rhymes and stories into action as he models his clay.

It is interesting to know that children under *seven* rarely model their clay from an object before them. They are primarily interested in reproducing the object as they see it in their own little minds. You can readily see how the child with an enriched background of both firsthand and story experiences will be more stimulated to express his ideas than the child who has had only a meager background of experiences. The carefully graded stories and authentic illustrations in My BOOK HOUSE will suggest many constructive activities to your child as he matures. He will want to model the interesting people, animals and objects with which he is familiar.

If the child has a sizeable lump of clay on his board when he begins to model animals or people, his finished object will be more

[1]The Gingerbread Man—B.H., II:58.
[2]The Story of Li'l' Hannibal—B.H., III:116.
[3]The Little Engine That Could—B.H., II:200.

[4]Little Jack Horner—B.H., I:48.
[5]Humpty Dumpty—B.H., I:46.

satisfying and substantial. Match sticks or toothpicks will help reinforce the legs of animals and people. Simply mold the clay over these sticks. Do not expect your child's first efforts with clay to be perfect. He will learn through handling the clay itself

how to smooth it here, pinch it off there, etc., to form the head and body of the figure he is attempting to model. If experimenting with clay gives your child an opportunity to express and clarify his own ideas and to learn to use his hands constructively, the experience will be well worth the effort.

Let Your Child Choose His Subject. It is best if the suggestions we give the child about his work grow out of his own interests and needs. The child of *two* or *three* gets real pleasure out of simply handling and changing the clay from one form to another. He rarely starts out to make a definite object. If the object he is making recalls something familiar to him, he may name it spontaneously. The same piece of clay will quickly become a ball, an apple, a tomato, or a balloon. The child identifies the main characteristics of the object as he names it. By flattening the clay with the palm of his hand, or putting a few holes in it with the tips of his fingers, he can quickly change it into the man in the moon or a table, etc.

By *five*, the child will be more interested in making concrete objects with his clay, and it is at this stage of his development that he begins to model simple bowls, animals, etc.

Modeling a Simple Bowl. Little children can model simple bowls and trays from a lump of clay. Give the child a lump of clay about the size of an apple to work with on his clay board. Let him roll

CLAY MODELING

the clay between the palms of his hands until it becomes a smooth ball-like mass. Place the ball of clay back on the clay board. The little child can easily make the opening of the bowl by pressing his fist into the center of the ball of clay. By gently squeezing and pushing this opening with his fingers and hands, he will learn to smooth it into the shape he desires. If cracks come in the clay, he can push them together again with his fingers. Moistening his hands in water will help him to smooth the outer surface of the bowl.

Coils of Clay. Pottery may also be made from coils of clay. Children from *seven* or *eight* years of age will have more success with this method of making pottery than will the younger child. Coils of clay are made by roll-  ing a piece of clay back and forth on the board with the palms of the hands.

The size of the coils used will depend on the size of the bowl to be made. Naturally, the larger the bowl, the thicker the coils of clay must be. Coils of about one-half inch thickness are practical for the average size bowl.

The base of the bowl may be made in several different ways. One way is to simply flatten the clay with a rolling pin until it is approximately the size you need. A cup or saucer placed upside down on the flattened clay will serve as a pattern for the base of

155

your bowl, and a dull knife can be used to cut around the edge. This circle of clay will serve as the base for your bowl. The base of your bowl may also be made from coils of clay. One-quarter or one-half inch coils are best for small bowls, while three-quarter or one-inch coils are more practical for larger bowls. To make the base, simply wind the coil round and round until you have the size base you need.

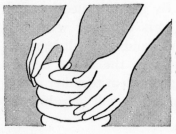

To build up the sides of the bowl, place a coil of clay directly on top of the outside edge of the base of the bowl. Build one row at a time, and join each clay coil together by gently pressing and molding it with your fingers until it is firm and smooth. Join the bottom edge of the first coil to the base of the bowl by molding and blending it with your fingers. Place the second row of coils directly on top of the row below, and join the bottom edge of this coil to the top edge of the coil below by molding and smoothing it with your fingers. Continue adding coils to your bowl until it is the right size.

You may want to narrow or widen the top of your bowl to give it a more interesting shape. To widen the bowl, simply place the last coil on the *outside* edge of the row below. To narrow the bowl, place the last coil on the *inside* edge of the row below.

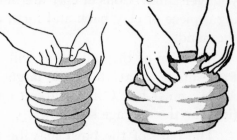

Moistening your fingers in water will help you to smooth the clay on the outside of the bowl. Keep the clay used for making coil pottery quite moist and the coils will stay pliable and bend easily.

CLAY MODELING

Handles and decorations are easily added to your bowl by pressing and molding them into the surface of the bowl. If these added pieces of clay are not joined securely, they will break off as soon as the clay is dry.

Coils of clay may also be used to make interesting designs, letters and numbers. The child who is learning to count and identify numbers and letters will enjoy using clay in this way.

To make clay numbers or letters, place a small lump of clay on the clay board and roll it back and forth with the palms of your hands until it forms a coil of clay. Twist and turn the coil into the shape of the letter or number.

Clay Plaques and Tiles. Plaques and tiles made of clay and decorated with a design or picture can be used as paper weights or pictures to hang on the wall. Begin with a lump of clay large enough to mold into a plaque or tile. These plaques or tiles may be round,

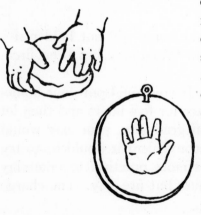

oval, square or oblong. The clay may be flattened with a rolling pin or the palms of your hands. A smooth stick or dull knife may be used to cut and shape your tile. Make your tile or plaque about one-half to three-quarters of an inch thick and it will be less likely to crack. If you plan to hang the tile or plaque on a wall, you will have to place a screw eye in the top of it while the clay is still moist.

157

IN YOUR HANDS

A design or picture traced in the clay while it is still moist will make the tile more interesting. A match stick, toothpick or hairpin may be used to draw on clay. Be sure to let your clay remain on the board until it is thoroughly dry. If your plaque is a large one, plan to keep the edges moist until the center is dry in order to prevent cracking. When the plaque or tile is completely dry, the design or picture may be put on with calcimine paint or enamel and given a coat of shellac.

HELPS IN WORKING WITH CLAY

Always allow your clay to remain on the board until thoroughly dry. (It takes clay at least twenty-four hours to dry. If the model is very thick, it may even take two or three days.)

After the clay is completely dry, take a fine piece of sandpaper and smooth off the rough spots. It is then ready for painting.

All colors of calcimine powder paint may be purchased inexpensively at any paint store.

To mix the paint, add equal parts of water and calcimine powder. This paint will rub off to a certain degree when dry. A coat of white shellac will put a hard finish on your clay and keep the clay and paint from rubbing off.

The older child may use enamel paint to give a glossy finish to his clay.

Firing Clay. The clay objects made at home will not hold water unless they have been fired in a kiln. When clay has been fired, water will not make it soft again.

It takes a whole day to fire clay. If you could put your homemade clay in the hot coals of a furnace for five hours and then let the fire die out and the clay cool off gradually, your clay would be fired. You can readily see how inconvenient it would be to try to fire your own clay at home. It is more practical to take clay objects to a kiln where they do nothing but fire clay. The charge for firing is very small.

CLAY MODELING

A Visit to the Pottery. The older child who enjoys working with clay will be interested in visiting a pottery. He will want to see the potter's wheel and watch the skill and precision of the potter as he molds plates and bowls on the turning wheel. He may even want to make a wheel to turn his own pottery at home. He will learn how pottery is glazed and fired into finished products. A trip like this will help build appreciation for the potter's skill and artistry.

Wedging Clay. At the pottery the child will also have an opportunity to see clay being wedged. He will learn how to wedge his own clay at home. Wedging is the name of the process used to remove airholes from clay to prevent cracking. Clay can be wedged at home by taking a lump of it and throwing it down on the clay board again and again until it becomes fine in texture and free from airholes.

Joining Clay with "Slip". At the pottery the child will also see huge pots of "slip" being used to cement one piece of clay on another. "Slip" is really just a solution of clay and water mixed until it is about the consistency of thick cream. The older child may want to try his own hand at joining parts of his clay with this mixture. A stiff brush is used to put the "slip" on the pieces of clay to be joined. The pieces are then pressed together and held firmly until the clay sets. Difficult pieces of pottery are easily made in this fashion.

Designs for Pottery. The child will be interested in decorating his clay with designs of his own. In the Index, Volume XII, of My BOOK HOUSE, you will find selections and illustrations listed that will suggest various designs for pottery, plaques and modeling.[6]

---

[6]See Unit No. 9, page 4, of *Creative Work for Your Child's Hands* for illustrations of pottery designs in My BOOK HOUSE.

IN YOUR HANDS

SUGGESTED CLAY ACTIVITIES

Pottery—Play dishes, ash trays, bowls, plates, etc.

Vases—Indian, Grecian, Egyptian, Spanish, etc.

Dishes to hold bulbs. Place a tin container inside the dish to hold the water.

Paper weights, plaques.[7]

Tiles representing the different countries—Dutch, Egyptian, etc.[8]

Candlesticks.

Animals, people and story characters.

Scenery—Trees, tunnels, etc.

Toy models.

Heads for puppets.

Fruits and vegetables.

Replicas of houses—Igloo, adobe, cave, etc.[8]

Statues and busts of Lincoln, Washington, etc.

Statue of Liberty—See B.H., XI:172.

In clay modeling, as in any other form of creative work, the child gets his inspiration from the things he sees and hears. Any experience he is exposed to that stimulates his imagination is sure to color his desire to express his thoughts and feelings in a creative way. The stories he hears and reads for himself, the information he has accumulated, the conversations he takes part in, the things he has seen, all help to give him ideas to express and an urge to create. Each finished product the child creates will add to his confidence and give him further proof of his own ability to do things with his hands.

See: [7]Unit No. 9, pages 2 and 5, *Creative Work for Your Child's Hands.*
  [8]Pictures and selections listed in Index of My BOOK HOUSE, Volume XII, page 235, under Countries of the World.
  Creative Expression on charts on pages 82 and 88 of IN YOUR HANDS.
  Creative Activities in Index of My BOOK HOUSE, Volume XII, page 283.

CHAPTER XIX

Happy Hours With Scissors, Cutting, Folding and Pasting

WHEN your child exhibits an active interest in scissors, it is wise to take the time to show him constructive ways to use them in order to prevent cutting mishaps.

By *two*, the little child has usually gained sufficient control of his hand muscles to learn to cut with scissors. The first scissors he uses should be blunt ones about five inches long, with blades that open and cut easily. Little hands are quite awkward when they handle scissors for the first time. It may be necessary to show the beginner how to operate them over and over again by placing his thumb in one loop and his third finger in the other one. It takes real effort and perseverance to learn to open and close the blades of the scissors so they will cut. There is a certain rhythm to cutting and snipping with scissors that the little child acquires only with experience.

Find a Use for His First Snippings. The beginner can practice cutting and snipping with newspapers. The child should have a definite place to do his cutting and pasting. If he has his own little work table, he will soon form the habit of going to it when he wants to carry on some activity. Likewise, if the child has been introduced to cutting with a special need in mind, he will come to associate scissors and cutting with constructive activities. It is a

161

IN YOUR HANDS

good idea to find some use for these first snippings the child cuts. He may want to fill a paper bag with them and glue the top closed to make a pillow or a pad for his teddy bear to rest on.

Talk flows freely with the little child who is cutting with scissors and he will want to tell you many things about the pieces of paper he cuts. They will represent many objects to him. Indeed, a square may be the house he lives in or a box filled with toys, while a circle may be a cookie or a rosy-cheeked apple! He will try his hand at pasting his snippings to make people, animals, houses, boats, airplanes, trains and fantastic designs. Cutting and pasting, like all creative activities, help give your child a feeling of confidence in his own ability to express himself.

Save Cutouts Until Later. If the little child has learned to handle scissors freely, he will come to think of his cutting as "drawing with scissors." The curves and turns on paper dolls and animal cutouts will be less difficult for him *after* he has learned to use his scissors for free cutting. Magazine pictures, paper dolls and other cutouts that require following a line, are suitable for the child who can manipulate his scissors with ease. Folding and pasting usually go hand in hand with cutting activities. Your child will spend many interesting

CUTTING AND PASTING

hours cutting pictures, illustrating his favorite stories, originating invitations and cards for birthday parties and celebrations, etc. He can make simple puppets by cutting out pictures of people and animals he has crayoned or painted.[1]

Children from *six* to *twelve* are interested in making paper dolls and designing costumes for them. At this age they also enjoy making posters of paper cutouts. The child will need to learn how to fold the paper in two in order to cut figures and designs. A knowledge of paper folding will make this cutting a much easier task and enable him to cut both sides of the paper at the same time.

Children find many uses for cutting and pasting. They will enjoy making:

Snowflakes.
Pin wheels.
Lacy designs and doilies.
Valentines.
Houses and buildings.
Paper dolls.
Doll clothes.
Figures of children and people.
Flowers, trees, sun, moon, etc.
Letters and numbers.
Birds and animals.
Fruits and vegetables.

Toy furniture.
Farm scenes and animals.
Scenery for puppet and shadow plays.
Favors and decorations for parties.
Cutouts.
Picture and design puzzles.
Patterns for woodworking and sewing.
Airplanes, boats, trains, cars, etc.
Story illustrations.
Scrapbooks with magazine pictures.

[1]See "Stick Puppets"—page 181 of this book.

IN YOUR HANDS

The following suggestions will help your child be more successful in his cutting, pasting and folding activities.

1. Have your child do his cutting and pasting at his own table.
2. Cover the table with a sheet of newspaper before he begins work.
3. Put a small quantity of soft paste in a jar that can be covered with a lid.
4. Provide a good paste brush that will stand washing.
5. Supply him with a clean cloth to pat down the picture he is pasting. The cloth will help to keep his work clean and prevent sticky fingers.
6. Teach him to place his picture face down on a clean newspaper before brushing the paste on it. Encourage him to use the paste cloth to pat the picture in place.

Stories and pictures and firsthand experiences will all offer inspiration and suggestions to the child for creative cutting and pasting. The Index in Volume XII of My BOOK HOUSE will help you quickly locate stories and pictures that will supplement your child's current interests. The following selections from My BOOK HOUSE indicate the type of rhyme, poem and story that lends itself well to cutting and pasting activities:

ANIMALS

See animal stories and illustrations listed in the Index, Volume XII, page 257 under Nature.

BIRDS

See bird stories and illustrations listed under Nature in Index, Volume XII, page 262.

FAMILIAR OBJECTS

Nursery rhymes and action rhymes abound in things familiar to the little child. See Rhymes in Index, Volume XII, page 273.

CUTTING AND PASTING

FARM ACTIVITIES

See stories and illustrations of horses, cows, pigs, barns, silos as well as activities listed under Farm and Country in Index, Volume XII, page 243. See also Unit No. 4 of *Creative Work for Your Child's Hands*.

NATURE

See stories and illustrations of flowers, trees, snow, rain, moon, stars, etc., listed in the Index of My BOOK HOUSE, Volume XII, page 257 under Nature. See also Unit No. 5 of *Creative Work for Your Child's Hands*.

PAPER DOLLS AND COSTUME DESIGNING

Suggestions for paper dolls, costume designing, scenery for puppet shows, etc., may be found on page 234 in the Index, Volume XII, under Costumes. See also Unit No. 3 of *Creative Work for Your Child's Hands*.

TRANSPORTATION

See selections listed under Transportation in Index, Volume XII, page 278. Illustrations of automobiles, boats, bridges, busses, steam shovels, trains, trucks give the child ideas that he can carry out with his scissors, paper and paste.

See Unit No. 1 of *Creative Work for Your Child's Hands*.

Give Your Child Crayon & Paint

L ONG before the child is able to express his ideas in words, he will attempt to portray them in crude form with paint and crayon. Both these mediums are attractive to him, and he will use them freely to express the fancies of his imagination. The pictures your child draws will represent his sincere efforts to record his feelings and impressions. He draws for the joy and satisfaction he feels in the activity and not because he wants to impress others with the results. If you will examine your child's painting and drawing with this understanding, you will become familiar with some of the intimate impressions he is forming about the world around him.

As early as *twelve* to *fifteen months*, the baby will reach for the pencil or crayon he sees the adult using. If this crayon is large enough for him to grasp in his little hands, he will try pounding it on the paper in an effort to make a mark. The same baby at *eighteen months* will

166

CRAYON AND PAINT

be able to use a crayon or long-handled easel brush to scribble or scrub on the paper. The little child is primarily interested in the activity paint and crayons provide, and the sense of power he feels in his own accomplishment pleases him greatly.

Drawing and Language Ability Go Hand in Hand. In this early stage, it is interesting to know that the little child's ability to express himself with paint and crayon will correspond closely with his power to use language. When he is in the scribble stage with his crayon or paint, he is also beginning to discard his babblings to repeat the few isolated words he is learning to say.

The Two and Three-Year-Old. By the time he is two, you can expect him to paint one color on top of another in his pictures. His scribblings will begin to emerge into circles and blotches, and while he sometimes names his drawings, he is more interested in the process of making them than in the results he achieves. It is not until the child is past three that we can recognize his drawings and be certain of interpreting them correctly. For this reason, it is best to ask the child to *tell you* about his pictures. This approach to his drawings will also encourage him to use the new words he is acquiring from day to day. Do not be alarmed if the two or three-year-old starts to tell you one thing about his picture and then, all of a sudden, changes his story. At this age and up until four, the child's imagination usually dictates the words he chooses to describe his experiences. The three-year-old enjoys moving his crayon back and forth across the paper in sweeping motions. It is a thrilling experience for him to be able to cover a piece of paper with color. A little later, he will call these strokes and blotches of color a sky, a road or whatever his fancy dictates at the time he is making them.

Drawings of Four-Year-Old Begin to Take on Form. Fantastic designs are popular with the young child, and they serve to represent many things to him. By four, the child's work should begin to take on form and meaning and be more readily recognized by adults, even though it is lacking in detail. If the three or four-year-old were to attempt to paint the elephant he has seen for the first time, his picture would probably be little more than the trunk and a scribble. The trunk of the elephant makes a tremendous impression on the child of this age. In fact, to his way of thinking, it *is the elephant*. Little children prefer bold colors to express their simple, sincere beliefs. You may be sure that the color the child chooses to paint his elephant will be far from its natural somber gray. Pictures created by the four-year-old will be treasured by him as prized possessions.

Drawings of Five-Year-Old Express Individuality. The five-year-old draws with a definite idea in mind. He is familiar with the names of colors and chooses them with great care. His drawings express his freedom or restraint, his imagination or lack of it, and his sense of neatness or disorder. The five-year-old's drawings are truly an

expression of his individuality rather than of his training, and so they will readily reveal his timidity or feeling of security.

Drawings Reveal Immaturity and Lack of Observation. If it is difficult for the parent to recognize the pictures the five-year-old is making, it is a fairly reliable indication that the child is immature for his age. The wise parent will plan to enrich his day with experiences and stories that will encourage the child to be more alert and accurate in his observations. At five, the child tries his hand at making people, houses, boats, trains, animals and even landscapes with trees, flowers, sun and moon. The details he considers most important will be drawn largest in his pictures. His paints and crayons will help him express experiences he has had at the zoo, circus, airport, etc., and you will discover he has learned many new words as he tells you the story of his pictures.

Drawing and painting give the child many opportunities to develop initiative and concentration. He will put forth tremendous effort to express a happy experience, and learn to coordinate his hand and mind as he begins to think things through logically. Parents can help promote creative ability in the child by developing his imagination and curiosity with a well-rounded background of graded literature that is colorfully illustrated. Interesting trips, and the presence of creative materials in the home will also help to stimulate the child's desire to create. The workings of his own imagination will supply him with an urgent desire to express himself. Let your child feel free to experiment with his crayons, paper and paint. The best role for a parent to play in directing the use of creative materials is that of a sympathetic shadow in the background. It is undoubtedly true that the more we attempt to *supervise* the child's creative ability, the more we *inhibit* it. Show your child the simple techniques he needs to use his materials freely. Place a large crayon or long-handled paint brush in his hand, provide him with large sheets of paper, set him at his own easel or work table and give him freedom to work out his own ideas as he chooses.

Color Books Tend to Inhibit Creativity. Drawing pictures for your child to copy may please him at the moment, but this practice is sure to rob him of his own initiative and originality. In fact, it may even stunt his own creative ability. Many of the color and paint books on the market do nothing toward developing his creative ability. Coloring inside these small outline pictures is really contrary to the large arm movement the child's muscular coordination requires. From *two* to *seven*, he needs large paper, thick crayons, and long-handled paint brushes to encourage the bold strokes that are best suited to the development of the big muscles in his arms and hands.

Emotional Reactions Reflected. The child's drawings should take on form as he matures and the parent should be able to observe mental growth in his pictures from month to month. The child's drawings may uncover many of his intimate thoughts and impressions that would otherwise be lost to the parent. His reaction to the new baby in the family, the robbery up the street, the parade he watched, are all bound to seep into his pictures, and the observant parent will be able to detect thoughts that are disturbing the child's feeling of security. His drawings may also reveal his need for understanding, encouragement and a richer background of firsthand experiences and stories.

The parent who is able to understand the child's creative efforts will be able to foster a fine relationship with his child. Creative ability is sure to grow and develop in a stimulating home environment. The child's imagination and his ability to reason will be greatly influenced by the mental food he is "fed" during his formative years. Creative materials in the home will inspire the imaginative child to satisfy his own natural desire to create.

Children Sensitive to Beauty Around Them. Children will unconsciously formulate their ideas of color harmony and beauty from the things they see around them. They become sensitive to the color combinations they see in nature and even to the colors in their clothing and picture books. Some children are naturally more sensitive to beauty and color than others, and so it is a good idea

CRAYON AND PAINT

to draw your child's attention to things that are particularly beautiful and attractive. When out walking, you might remark about the lovely green of the grass, the blue of the water in the lake, or the cheerful song of the robin. All these experiences will encourage an awareness and appreciation for beauty in your child. Let him help arrange the flowers for your table, decide on the color of socks, handkerchief and tie that goes best with his suit. It is through simple everyday experiences like these that the little child becomes conscious of the beauty around him. Make it a special treat to visit a flower show or the art department of your favorite store. If you are visiting the art gallery or museum, be careful not to bore him with detailed information beyond his interest and understanding. The little child develops an appreciation for beauty and color from the things he sees around him, and his ability to appreciate beauty and harmony is influenced by his everyday environment.

Some simple equipment and materials that will help set the stage for the growth of free expression in your child's painting and drawing are listed below.

PAINTING

Easel.

Several long-handled brushes—about 12 inches long. A good assortment includes a ¼, ½, and ¾-inch bristle. Calcimine powder paint—powdered calcimine may be purchased inexpensively at any paint store. It is well to start with one or two colors. Red, blue, yellow and brown are good basic colors. The powder paint can be mixed as needed. Empty half-pint mayonnaise jars that can be covered with a lid are fine for keeping the paint fresh. It is best to mix it in small quantities. One part calcimine powder to two parts water makes a satisfactory mixture. Stir the powder and water with a stick until it is well mixed.

Pad of unprinted newspaper for easel—18 by 24 inches. Wrapping paper or wallpaper used on the reverse side.

171

Smock or coverall for child. Cloth to wipe paint off brushes. Small wash basin and cloth for child to use to wash easel and brushes when finished painting. Thumb tacks to fasten paper on easel.

Twine, or clothesline to hang paintings on until dry, and clothespins.

DRAWING

Large sheets of wrapping paper saved from packages. Pad of unprinted newspaper—18 by 24 inches—sold especially for easel drawing.

Sheets of wrapping paper or unprinted newspaper may be pasted together for friezes, wall hangings, scenery, etc.

Large wax crayons—assorted colors.

Colored chalk.

Thick pencil.

Charcoal.

SUGGESTIONS THAT WILL HELP YOUR CHILD HANDLE HIS PAINTS AND CRAYONS MORE SKILLFULLY.

1. Place newspapers on floor under easel before starting to paint.
2. Fasten paper to easel with thumb tacks to hold it securely.
3. Encourage the child to use large arm movements for crayoning and painting. (Sheets of paper, 18 by 24 inches, allow him more freedom to do this.)
4. Wipe excess paint off brush by pressing it against the side of the jar. (This prevents runs that spoil his pictures.)
5. Hang freshly painted pictures on line to dry. Wooden pinch-type clothespins will hold the paper securely and are easy for the child to handle.
6. Use a basin, cloth and water to wash the easel and brushes each time they are used.
7. Place lids on jars to prevent paint from drying when not in use.

CRAYON AND PAINT

Mixing Colors. The child from *five* to *seven* is ready to learn to mix his own color combinations. Let him mix red and blue and discover he has purple. Show him how to make orange, by mixing red and yellow; green, by mixing blue and yellow; and gray, by mixing black and white.

Allan—age 6.

Children like to draw and paint favorite characters and scenes from their stories. The child's pictures will express more originality if we do not try to suggest patterns of conventional people or objects to him.

Friezes and posters are a favorite of children from kindergarten on through high school. They may be painted or crayoned on

strips of wrapping paper or unprinted newspaper. Older children may want to choose muslin or oilcloth to make a more permanent frieze. This type of activity belongs to children of kindergarten age and above. As a rule, two or more children will paint on the frieze at the same time. Friezes and posters

173

adapt themselves well to social studies in school. A frieze depicting Colonial life, Indian life and life in other lands, will give the child a splendid opportunity to record many of the interesting customs he has read about in his studies.

The more opportunities you give your child to work out his own ideas with creative materials, the greater his appreciation will become for the work of fine artists. Your child's imagination will be limited only by his acquaintanceship with life as it is unfolded to him through his experiences, rhymes, stories and picture books. Feed the child's imagination, and he will possess the spark that will best fire his own desire to create!

REFERENCES

See: Creative Expression on charts—pages 82 and 88 of IN YOUR HANDS.

Selections listed in Index of My BOOK HOUSE, Volume XII, under Artists and Illustrators, page 227, and Creative Activities, page 283.

Packet of *Creative Work for Your Child's Hands.*

Holidays Begin at Home

THE little child gathers meaning of the holidays from the association woven around them in his own home. It is difficult for him to grasp the significance of Christmas, Easter, Fourth of July, etc., unless he has a meaningful part in their celebration. Holidays should bring the family very close together and provide an opportune time for everyone to work and plan for a happy occasion. Little children will enter into the holiday spirit if they are allowed to help make cookies, candy, favors, place cards, decorations for the house and table, and arrange the program of the day.

Some holidays are ones for reverence, like Christmas, Easter and Thanksgiving, and the celebration should suit the spirit of the holiday. Others are ones of obligation and respect, and the child will enter into this spirit only if the parent plants the significant thought in the child's initial celebration. New Years' Day, St. Valentine's Day and Hallowe'en are truly happy fun-making occasions for children, and the simplicity with which they are celebrated will enhance the memory of them.

Stories and pictures help the little child begin his appreciation of holidays and bring them into his sphere of understanding. The story of Abraham Lincoln and the robins[1] will give the child a friendly feeling toward the great statesman and make him eager to know more about his kindness and generosity. The little child will begin to build his ideas of Flag Day when he hears the story of "George Washington and the First American Flag."[2] The red, white and blue of his flag will mean more to him when he knows the names of the colors and why they were chosen. Begin with simple truths that the child can understand, and add to these from time to time as he grows and matures.

[1] A Story About Abe Lincoln—B.H., V:129.
[2] B.H., V:116.

IN YOUR HANDS

Music and song will also help the child capture the spirit of the holidays.[3] Christmas carols and church bells, marches and national music, and the weird music of witches and goblins add an intangible quality to Christmas, Fourth of July and Hallowe'en.

A holiday may be just a day off or it may have real significance to your child according to the way he is introduced to it in the home.

REFERENCES

For holiday selections in My BOOK HOUSE, see Index, Volume XII, page 248.

See also Unit No. 6 of *Creative Work for Your Child's Hands.*

[3]See chapter Let Your Child Discover the Joy of Music, page 187.

CHAPTER XXII

Dramatic Play

IF you would have your child grow in poise, develop originality, initiative and a sense of responsibility, be sure to encourage his efforts at dramatic play. Dramatization that is free and spontaneous is natural and pleasing to the child. It gives him another outlet through which he may actively express his feelings and enthusiasm.

The *tiny baby* begins to imitate the actions of the people around him long before he has learned to say words. He loves to "patty cake" after mother, shake his hand for "bye, bye," and move his arms apart when you say, "so big" to him. A little later on he will try his hand at writing with any object that looks like the pencil he has seen you using, pretend to read from a book, and delight in toddling around the house performing everyday chores he has seen mother or daddy doing. The little girl seeks every opportunity to try on mother's hats and shoes or use "make-up;" while the little man of the house is trying to fix the doorknobs or plumbing in the same manner he has seen daddy repair them.

Up until *three*, children are unconsciously dramatizing the *actions* of the people around them. By the time the child is three, his vocabulary is usually sufficient for him to attempt to imitate the *language* of others as well as to express some of his own ideas.

177

IN YOUR HANDS

He loses himself entirely in his dramatic play and puts forth tremendous effort to make his role realistic. The little child learns to make many desirable social adjustments as he imitates mother or father in his own daily activities.

If you will place a few discarded hats, high heeled slippers, boots, a wooden sword, a shawl, a cane, a high silk hat, some long trousers, and a discarded party dress in a box or chest in the child's playroom or attic, he will joyously enter into simple childlike dramatic play. The little child does not need scenery to make his play-acting sincere. His imagination can quickly change the discarded party dress into the raiment of a beautiful princess or the cane into a magic wand. If the child's imagination has been developed with a background of desirable stories and experiences, he will possess all the magic necessary to turn the family dog into a fine white charger or a human playmate. My BOOK HOUSE will enable you to give your child the story background he needs to awaken his interest and inspire his thinking.

Dramatic play will give the "only child" and the timid child opportunities to *feel* the courage and confidence of the character he is impersonating.

The Child Remembers Best What He Learns Dramatically. When he has had an active part in the "doing" of things, he has really learned dramatically. Educators have long made use of this principle of learning, and the activity programs in schools are built around this very thought. When your first-grader tells you he is building a home, post office, firehouse or airport at school, and your older boy mentions that he is carding wool or building a replica of a colonial mansion in his classroom, you will understand that these activities are planned to make his studies more interesting and meaningful. All these activities will help him to develop cooperative social qualities and enable him to fit more gracefully into his part of living and working with others. In order to be a good postman, your child must first become familiar with the duties and responsibilities of the man who delivers the mail. He will seek information and stories that will tell him more about the postman in order to excel in his role.

Dramatic play will make your child more conscious of the qualities of good speech. The reading he does to gather information on each new activity will bring him in contact with many new words that he will want to use in his dramatic play.

Parents Have the Privilege of Encouraging Dramatic Play at Home. The family group provides an excellent cast for dramatizing stories from nursery rhymes to the plays of Shakespeare. Stories of the finest literary quality lend themselves best to dramatization. Encourage your child to try his hand at playing many characters in the same story. Children are not ready to give a dramatization of a story until they are thoroughly familiar with the part each character plays. Dramatization is really the *culmination* of literary experiences and not the means of introducing the child to literature.

Little children enjoy acting out a favorite scene from a familiar story, and it is better to let the child give his own spontaneous interpretation than to coach and rehearse him in the lines of the story. When he is old enough to feel the need for organized play acting, let him have an active part in all the planning concerning costumes, scenery, etc. The little child is not concerned with settings and properties, and these details may hamper his pleasure and spontaneity. He is interested in dramatizing familiar nursery

rhymes and parts of well loved stories like *The Gingerbread Man,
Little Black Sambo*, or *Goldilocks and the Three Bears*, etc.[1]

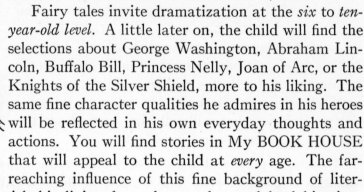

Fairy tales invite dramatization at the *six* to *ten-year-old level.* A little later on, the child will find the selections about George Washington, Abraham Lincoln, Buffalo Bill, Princess Nelly, Joan of Arc, or the Knights of the Silver Shield, more to his liking. The same fine character qualities he admires in his heroes will be reflected in his own everyday thoughts and actions. You will find stories in My BOOK HOUSE that will appeal to the child at *every* age. The far-reaching influence of this fine background of literature will enrich his living from day to day and lead him into many interesting hobbies.

Homemade shadow plays, movies and puppet shows[2] will be enjoyed by every member of the family from the toddler on!

Homemade Movies. Children enjoy making their own movies about a favorite story or experience. They may begin by drawing or painting a series of pictures on sheets of paper identical in size. These pictures are then assembled and pasted on a long sheet of paper to make the "film." The film is wound on two wooden rollers and placed in the movie box.

Children enjoy playing the role of announcer as the film unfolds. When they are learning to read, the home-made movie will stimulate their desire to read parts of the story from the book. Older boys and girls will delight in writing original stories and plays for their movie theater.

[1]See Selections in My BOOK HOUSE for Encouraging Imitation and Dramatic Play in Your Child, listed on page 184 of this book.

[2]For other suggestions—see Unit No. 12 of *Creative Work for Your Child's Hands.*

DRAMATIC PLAY

Puppets and Marionettes. Puppets and marionettes fascinate children of all ages. They may be as crude or artistic as the child is capable of making them.

The hand puppet is easily managed by the child of *five* or *six* and will quickly take on the personality of the child operating it. Here is a pattern for a simple hand puppet that the child operates by placing his thumb in one arm and his third finger in the other one. The head of the puppet is operated by the index finger. The hand puppet should be made to suit the hand-spread of the child who is to use it. Yarn may be used for the puppet's hair, and his eyes, nose and mouth may be painted, crayoned, or sewed on with stitching and buttons.

The child *under six* can make puppets by cutting out pictures he has drawn on cardboard or heavy paper. These figures may be nailed or glued on a stick and used as stick puppets.

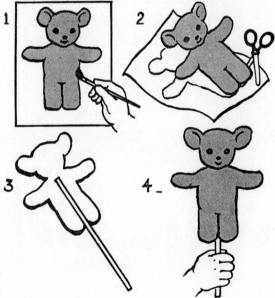

The older child will be interested in making puppets similar to those suggested in the "Puppet" unit included in the envelope of *Creative Work for Your Child's Hands*.

The size of the puppets will depend upon the age of the child using them and the size of the stage. Large puppets, about fifteen or sixteen inches tall, are best for young children as they bring their big hand muscles into play.

Children from fourth grade on through high school will get a great deal of pleasure from making their own puppet and marionette shows. Puppet plays inspire the designing of costumes and scenery to fit the period and nationality of the characters. Puppet enthusiasts will read widely in the field of literature, history and art to find the information they need to make their puppets authentic in every detail.

The puppet stage may be a simple wooden box with muslin curtains or an elaborate theater, depending on the maturity of the child making and using it. The little child will operate his stick puppets from below the floor level of the puppet theater, while the older child will learn to operate string puppets from the space at the top of the stage.

Puppets and marionettes provide the child with another avenue of expression and help him see the need for clear speech. They also help develop the child's personality. Many children who would otherwise hesitate to perform before a group seem to find the confidence to express themselves freely through the puppet characterization.

DRAMATIC PLAY

Shadow Plays. Shadow plays may be simple or complex according to the age and interests of the children taking part in them.

A screen is required to produce shadow plays. A sheet, a transparent window shade or a movie screen, will serve the purpose. The size of the screen will depend on the size of the silhouettes used for the characters in your play. If you want to give human shadow plays, the screen must be large enough to reflect the child's silhouette.

The screen may be hung over a doorway or put on a roller to be raised and lowered when needed. The space at the bottom of the screen should be covered with heavy material or cardboard. Place the cardboard high enough so that the "actor" will be concealed from the audience as he manipulates the puppet. Place an electric light behind the screen to reflect the silhouette of the actor or puppet as he comes between the light and the screen.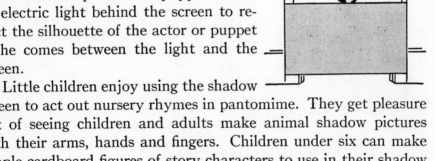

Little children enjoy using the shadow screen to act out nursery rhymes in pantomime. They get pleasure out of seeing children and adults make animal shadow pictures with their arms, hands and fingers. Children under six can make simple cardboard figures of story characters to use in their shadow plays.

Shadow plays offer the child unlimited possibilities for creative expression in play writing and the making and designing of scenery and costumes.

183

IN YOUR HANDS

Selections in My BOOK HOUSE for Encouraging Imitation and Dramatic Play in Your Child

Suggestions for the Young Child

D R A M A T I C   P L A Y

IN YOUR HANDS

Suggestions for the Older Child

For additional references in My BOOK HOUSE, see Index, Volume XII—Games and Rhythms, page 245—Plays and Pageants, page 271—Puppets, Marionettes and Shadow Plays, page 272 and Unit No. 12 of *Creative Work for Your Child's Hands.*

Let Your Child Discover the Joy of Music

CHAPTER XXIII

Your child is never too young to hear good music—to hear the sound of beautiful lullabies softly crooned and played. Music should be a part of his daily experience, for rhythm and sound are more primitive than language itself. Baby possesses a sense of rhythm from birth. He senses it in the actions of others and expresses it in his own bodily movements. Music reflects the moods and feelings of humanity—it is, indeed, the "universal language."

Your child need not possess the potential qualities of a musician in order to enjoy music. He will discover music by hearing it— much in the same manner as he discovers languáge. The child must hear and experience music and song before he is ready to express himself musically. Let his first experience with music be that of hearing beautiful lullabies and he will always treasure the memory of them. The young baby soon learns to imitate the tunes he hears mother hum as she goes about her daily tasks. He learns to sing, as he learns to talk, through listening and imitation. Music will help your child express his thoughts and feelings. He should be encouraged to sing and express himself rhythmically for the sheer joy it affords him and not merely for exhibition purposes.

Children Express Rhythm in Many Ways. They express it in bodily movements, words and tunes, etc. The little boy hammering nails in a board might well express his feeling of the rhythm by accompanying each bang of the hammer with a sing-songy *bing-bang,*

187

bing-bang. The youngster on the see-saw may be inspired to rhythmic expression with an *up-down, up-down,* or a *bump-up, bump-up,* as he enjoys his ride.

By *eighteen months* babies hum spontaneously or sing syllables in a rhythmic manner. They are alert to sounds; whistles, bells and clocks attract their attention. By *twenty-four months* they can usually sing a phrase of a song they have heard, although it may not always be on pitch. The child of this age loves a rocking horse or a rocking chair, and somehow these rocking movements seem to inspire him to express himself in song and rhythm. He may seek ways to express his feeling of rhythm through such bodily movements as nodding his head, swinging his arms, tapping his feet, or by going around bending his knees in a bouncing motion.

Be sure that the songs and music your child hears are suitable for his impressionable little mind. The melodies and poetry should be of the best, and the thought and meaning on the child's own level of understanding.

Mother Finds Many Ways to Introduce Song in the Little Child's Day. By *three* he is ready to match simple tones. When mother calls him she may sing his name rather than call it, and he, in return, may imitate mother's tune with, "I'm here!"

Ro-bert   I'm here!

Many of the animal sounds may be sung to the child to encourage tone matching. For example:

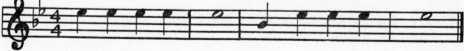

Cock -a - doo - dle doo! Good morn-ing to   you!

The *three-year-old* can generally sing short songs, although again he may not always be on pitch. He enjoys experimenting with musical instruments and can walk, run, gallop and jump to music in fairly good time.

The child of *four* is interested in dramatizing songs and enjoys "singing games"[1] like, *Ring Around a Rosy, The Farmer in the Dell, Lazy Old Mary,* etc. Children at this age often find delight in teasing other children by singing nicknames or chants similar to, "c-r-y--baby, c-r-y--baby," "Georgie has a g-i-r-l," etc.

By *five* the child is ready to sing a melody on pitch and to recognize and appreciate a number of songs and tunes. He can skip with music, hop on one foot, and dance rhythmically. By listening he discovers that music can be loud or soft, fast or slow, and attempts to interpret it with steps of his own.

Children enjoy hearing and examining instruments played by others. They like to imitate the motions used in playing these instruments and supply their own sound effects.

Homemade Instruments.[2] Rhythm sticks, musical comb, tom-tom, rattle or a scale of glasses tuned with varying amounts of water, are a means of introducing your child to rhythm and music. The soft tone of the homemade tom-tom is far more suitable to his thin voice than the sound of an expensive commercial drum.

See: [1]Selections listed under Games and Rhythms in My BOOK HOUSE, Index, Volume XII, page 245.
[2]Unit No. 11 of *Creative Work for Your Child's Hands.*

IN YOUR HANDS

A homemade xylophone or scale of spoons will interest the child and encourage him to make up simple tunes of his own for his favorite rhymes or poems.

Music Can Play Important Part in Child's Life. Radios and motion pictures have brought the great orchestras, fine artists and operas within the reach of every family. During his early years expose your child to good music and opportunities to express himself in a rhythmic fashion. The time to begin formal music training varies with the individual child and depends largely on his muscular development and his own desire to acquire the necessary skill. However, the child who is familiar with good music will have a greater incentive to persevere and practice until he has learned to play the instrument that appeals to him. Good music in the home will help reveal any inherent musical talent your child may possess.

Stories of musical compositions will add to the child's interest and appreciation of music. My BOOK HOUSE Plan has included a background of lullabies, folk songs, and stories of musical composers and their compositions to help you stimulate the love for good music in your child. In the Index, Volume XII, on page 254 under "Music," you will find many musical tales from other lands. The story illustrations picture the characters in their native costumes and add color and meaning to the music your child hears.

There are many fine records on the market made especially for children. Beginning on page 195 of this book you will find the monthly Calendars with the names of famous musicians. These lists of musicians include a specific BOOK HOUSE reference for every composition given. With this background of stories the child who hears Liszt's

THE JOY OF MUSIC

Hungarian Rhapsody is better equipped to appreciate the gaiety and spontaneity of the gypsy influence in Hungarian music. The illustrations accompanying the story of Bratton's *The Teddy Bears' Picnic* (Volume II, page 57), will help your child visualize the cumbersome bears walking when he hears the strongly accented rhythm of the music. If he is familiar with Humperdinck's version of the opera *Hansel and Grethel* (Volume VI, page 11), he will be ready to identify the weird strains of music as the witch, and the gay stacatto phrases of the score as the dancing of the fairies and brownies. The child who has heard Chopin's *Little Dog Waltz* (Volume II, page 150), will find added delight in the music as he imagines the little dog whirling around and around trying to catch his tail. A background of stories tends to add atmosphere and third dimension to the music your child hears.

Music will help your child form the habit of listening. Through listening he discovers music may be loud or soft, high or low, graceful or sturdy, and these details help him interpret the thought and mood of the composition. When he has learned this, he will readily understand why he must listen and let the music talk. Music will do much to give your child freedom, joy and happiness. If he is able to feel the freedom of song and expression he will have a better appreciation of the beauty around him and grow in emotional poise and satisfaction.

See "Music" on various charts—pages 80 to 105 of this book.
See selections under "Music" in Index of My BOOK HOUSE, Volume XII—page 254.
See suggestions on Music and Composers in Calendar.

CALENDAR OF EVENTS

for the

Twelve Months of the Year

with

References to Appropriate
Material Contained

in

My BOOK HOUSE Plan

In the Calendar, the following key of references has been used: B. H., 3:111 means My BOOK HOUSE, Volume 3, page 111; *Comment* indicates that particular mention has been made to the person or event in the text of the page listed; *Note* refers to a footnote at the bottom of the designated page; and *Biog.* is the abbreviation used for biography.

Special Events and Famous People in
My BOOK HOUSE who were born in the month of

MUSICIANS

22nd—Leon Jessel (1871-   )
German Composer
B.H., 6:111 *Note*

27th—Wolfgang Mozart (1756-1791)
Austrian Composer
B.H., 3:42 *Note*   B.H., 6:159 *Biog.*

31st—Franz Peter Schubert (1797-1828)
Austrian Composer
B.H., 2:26 *Note*   B.H., 3:161 *Note*

OTHER FAMOUS PEOPLE

1st—Betsy Ross (1752-1836)
Traditional Maker of the First American Flag
B.H., 5:116 *Comments*

4th—Charles E. Stratton (1838-1883)
American Dwarf
B.H., 8:150 *Comment*
B.H., 8:155

12th—Edmund Burke (1729-1797)
British Statesman
B.H., 12:40 *Comment*

19th—David Starr Jordan (1851-1931)
First President of Leland Stanford University
B.H., 6:127

19th—James Watt (1736-1819)
British Inventor and Engineer—discoverer
of the power of steam
B.H., 5:45 *Biog.*

19th—Robert E. Lee (1807-1870)
Commander-in-Chief of the Confederate
Army; College President
B.H., 5:136 *Comment*

29th—William McKinley (1843-1901)
Twenty-Fifth President of the United States
and Officer in the Civil War
B.H., 9:77 *Comment*

SPECIAL EVENTS IN JANUARY

1st—New Year's Day
B.H., 3:45   B.H., 8:92

1st—The Emancipation Proclamation freeing the slaves was
issued in 1863 by President Lincoln.
B.H., 5:129, 137

24th—Gold Discovered in California
Kit Carson acted as a guide to convoy gold-seekers to the Pacific
Coast in 1849-50.
B.H., 9:30   B.H., 12:143

Special Events and Famous People in
My BOOK HOUSE who were born in the month of

FEBRUARY

22nd—Frédéric Chopin (1810-1849)
Polish Composer
B.H., 2:150

**23rd—George Frederick Händel
(1685-1759)**
German Composer
B.H., 7:73, 119

24th—Arrigo Boito (1842-1918)
Italian Composer
B.H., 12:168

28th—John Alden Carpenter (1876-   )
American Composer
B.H., 2:172
Notes: B.H., 3:182, 183, 185

**29th—Gioachino Antonio Rossini
(1792-1868)**
Italian Composer
B.H., 10:44

OTHER FAMOUS PEOPLE

2nd—Daniel Boone (1734-1820)
American Pioneer
B.H., 9:7 *Biog.*

6th—Anne (1665-1714)
Queen of Great Britain and Ireland
B.H., 12:32, 107 *Note*

12th—Abraham Lincoln (1809-1865)
Sixteenth President of the United States
B.H., 5:128, 129 *Biog.*, 137
Comments: B.H., 8:171
B.H., 12:117, 137

19th—David Garrick (1717-1779)
Great English Actor
"One of the most famous actors that ever
lived." Buried in Westminster Abbey be-
neath the Monument to Shakespeare
B.H., 12:40 *Comment*

22nd—George Washington (1732-1799)
First President of the United States
B.H., 5:116 *Biog.*
Comments: B.H., 8:144, 146
B.H., 9:12
B.H., 12:113, 135

**26th—William Frederick Cody
(1845-1917)**
American Frontiersman, Scout and Showman
Familiarly known as "Buffalo Bill"
B.H., 9:30 *Biog.*

SPECIAL EVENTS IN FEBRUARY

14th—St. Valentine's Day
B.H., 1:86, 209   B.H., 3:198

18th—Bunyan's "Pilgrim's Progress" Published, 1678
Considered the greatest religious treatise in the world—translated
into 100 languages and dialects—more than any other book
except the Bible
B.H., 12:32 *Note*
Comments: B.H., 12: 128, 162

25th—Capture of Vincennes, Indiana
By Colonel George Rogers Clark, 1779
B.H., 9:66

—— —Brotherhood Week
Always includes Washington's birthday; the Sunday nearest Feb-
ruary 22nd is Brotherhood Day
Its objective is "justice, amity, understanding and cooperation
among Protestants, Catholics and Jews."
B.H., 9:129   B.H., 11:172, 173

Special Events and Famous People in
My BOOK HOUSE who were born in the month of

ARTISTS AND ILLUSTRATORS

5th—Peter Newell (1862-1924)
American Illustrator and Humorist
B.H., 4:118   B.H., 6:69

5th—Howard Pyle (1853-1911)
American Illustrator, Painter and Author
B.H., 8:132

**6th—Michelangelo Buonarroti
(1475-1564)**
Italian Painter, Sculptor, Architect and Poet
B.H., 6:164 *Note*

17th—Kate Greenaway (1846-1901)
English Illustrator and Poetess
B.H., 1:150, 151
B.H., 3:26, 27, 62 *Note*, 163 *Note*

22nd—Randolph Caldecott (1846-1886)
English Artist, Illustrator of Children's Books
B.H., 3:62, 163 *Note*   B.H., 5:76

22nd—Sir Anthony Van Dyck (1599-1641)
Flemish Painter
Tales Told in Holland: 157, 158

27th—Nathaniel Currier (1813-1888)
American Lithographer and Publisher of
    Prints
With James Merritt Ives (1824-1895) he
    formed the famous firm of Currier and Ives,
    "print-makers to the American people."
    Their prints furnished a pictorial record of
    all phases of the American life of their time
    and are now collectors' items.
B.H., 5:116, 117 *Pictures, Notes*

AUTHORS, DRAMATISTS AND POETS

1st—William Dean Howells (1837-1920)
American Printer, Journalist, Editor, Poet
B.H., 5:54

**6th—Elizabeth Barrett Browning
(1806-1861)**
English Poetess
B.H., 1:143, 185   B.H., 12:94 *Biog.*
B.H., 2:138

12th—Mary Howitt (1799-1888)
English Author
B.H., 5:111

16th—Emile Cammaerts (1878-   )
Belgian Poet
B.H., 2:141

19th—William Allingham (1824-1889)
Irish Poet
B.H., 3:94

20th—Henrik Ibsen (1828-1906)
Norwegian Dramatist
B.H. 9:98

23rd—Madison Cawein (1865-1914)
American Poet
B.H., 2:41

**30th—Raymond MacDonald Alden
(1873-1924)**
American Author and Educator
B.H., 7:173

7th—Maurice Ravel (1875-1937)
French Composer
B.H., 6:224 *Note*

8th—Ruggiero Leoncavallo (1858-1919)
Italian Composer
B.H., 2:143 *Note*

11th—Antonio Bazzini (1818-1897)
Italian Composer
B.H., 4:149 *Note*

12th—Thomas Arne (1710-1778)
English Musician and Composer
B.H., 10:165 *Note*

18th—Nikolai Rimski-Korsakov
(1844-1908)
Russian Composer
B.H., 4:73 *Note*   B.H., 8:93 *Note*
B.H., 7:91 *Note*

21st—Johann Sebastian Bach
(1685-1750)
German Composer
B.H., 9:134 *Note*
B.H., 12:185 *Note*

21st—Thurlow Lieurance (1878-   )
American Composer
B.H., 9:93 *Note*

31st—Joseph Haydn (1732-1809)
Austrian Composer; Originator of the Symphony
B.H., 3:42 *Note*

SPECIAL EVENTS IN MARCH

4th—George Washington Became First President of the United States, although not inaugurated until April 30th.
B.H., 5:125 *Comment*

17th—St. Patrick's Day
For selections see *Countries of the World–Ireland* in Index, Volume 12

23rd—Patrick Henry Delivered His Famous Speech containing the challenge "give me liberty or give me death."
B.H., 9:67 *Comment*

———— Vernal Equinox—the point at which the center of the sun moves across the celestial equator from south to north.
Marks the beginning of Spring in the northern hemisphere and occurs about March 21st—"Equinox" from the Latin for equal night, signifies the time of the year when day and night are equal.
For selections see *Spring* under *Nature–Seasons* in Index, Volume 12.

Special Events and Famous People in
My BOOK HOUSE who were born in the month of

29th—**Edward Rowland Sill** (1841-1888)
American Scholar and Poet
B.H., 6:201   B.H., 10:18

MUSICIANS

3rd—**Charles René de Boisdeffre**
(1838-1906)
French Composer
B.H., 3:161 *Note*

3rd—**Reginald De Koven** (1861-1920)
American Composer—Especially of Light
  Opera
B.H., 11:49

13th—**Félicien David** (1810-1876)
French Musician and Composer
B.H., 3:173 *Note*

OTHER FAMOUS PEOPLE

2nd—**Charlemagne, Emperor of the
Franks** (742-814 A.D.)
Soldier, Ruler and Patron of Learning

B.H., 10:38   B.H., 12:225 *Comment*
Tales Told in Holland: 94

16th—**Wilbur Wright** (1867-1912)
Inventor and Manufacturer of Airplanes
B.H., 5:66

23rd—**Stephen A. Douglas** (1813-1861)
Known for His Public Debates with Abraham
  Lincoln
B.H., 5:134 *Comment, Picture, Note*

25th—**William I, the Silent, Prince of
Orange** (1533-1584)
Founder of the Dutch Republic
Tales Told in Holland: 125, 138, 144

25th—**Oliver Cromwell** (1599-1658)
English Soldier and Statesman
B.H., 1:45 *Note*
B.H., 12:29 *Note*, 220 *Comment*

26th—**John James Audubon** (1785-1851)
American Naturalist; Pioneer Ornithologist;
  Born in Haiti and Educated in France
For selections see *Nature–Birds* in Index,
  Volume 12.

SPECIAL EVENTS IN APRIL

1st—**April Fool's Day**
Tales Told in Holland: 134 *Comment*

3rd—**First Pony Express Riders Left Sacramento, California**
to ride east and St. Joseph, Missouri to ride west—1860.
William F. Cody was one of the riders.
B.H., 9:30

14th—**Abraham Lincoln Assassinated**
Lincoln was shot on April 14, 1865 and died the following day.
B.H., 5:136 *Comment*

14th—**Pan-American Day**
Observed annually by the twenty-one American republics since 1931
For selections see *Mexico* and *South America* under *Countries of the
  World* in Index, Volume 12.

——— —**Easter Sunday**
Celebrated the first Sunday after the full moon that appears on or
  following the vernal equinox (March 21st). Easter moves between
  March 22nd and April 25th.
For selections see *Holidays–Easter*, and *Spring* under *Nature–Seasons*
  in Index, Volume 12.

Special Events and Famous People in
My BOOK HOUSE who were born in the month of

203

31st—Walt Whitman (1819-1892)
American Poet
B.H., 2:45
B.H., 12:136, 137 *Comments*, 153 *Note*

MUSICIANS

7th—Johannes Brahms (1833-1897)
German Composer and Pianist
B.H., 2:26 *Note*   B.H., 7:11 *Note*
B.H., 4:159 *Note*

7th—Peter Tchaikovsky (1840-1893)
Russian Composer
B.H., 2:218
Notes: B.H., 4:65, 145
    B.H., 6:19
    B.H., 8:18
    B.H., 10:98
    B.H., 11:162

12th—Jules Massenet (1842-1912)
French Composer
B.H., 10:109 *Note*

15th—Michael Balfe (1808-1870)
Irish Composer
B.H., 8:188 *Note*

22nd—Richard Wagner (1813-1883)
German Composer
B.H., 4:192 *Note*
B.H., 5:162 *Note*, 178 *Comment*, 179 *Note*
B.H., 7:72 *Note*
B.H., 10:11 *Note*, 89
B.H., 11:73

OTHER FAMOUS PEOPLE

11th—Johnny Appleseed (John Chapman) (1768-1847)
Picturesque Pioneer who planted apple seeds throughout our Middle West
B.H., 4:213

24th—Victoria (1819-1901)
Queen of Great Britain and Ireland and Empress of India
B.H., 8:155
Comments: B.H., 12:54, 65, 107
Notes: B.H., 10:54
    B.H., 12:107, 109, 113

29th—Patrick Henry (1736-1799)
Statesman and Orator; Signer of the Declaration of Independence
B.H., 5:120, 121 *Picture, Comment*
B.H., 9:67 *Comment*

SPECIAL EVENTS IN MAY

1st—May Day
The first of May has been a festival of merrymaking, dancing, and flowers from earliest times. Its observance probably grew out of the natural joy at the arrival of Spring.
For selections on May Day see *Holidays–May Day* and *Nature–Flowers* in Index, Volume 12.
Nursery Friends from France: 146, 147, 152, 153, 154, 172
See also Unit No. 6 of *Creative Work for Your Child's Hands.*

16th—Joan of Arc Day
France observes this day in honor of the little French heroine.
B.H., 10:98

17th—Norwegian Independence Day, marking the adoption of the constitution of Norway, 1814
See selections listed under *Countries of the World–Norway* in Index, Volume 12.

18th—World Good-Will Day
This date marked the opening of the first Hague Peace Conference in 1899, which established the Permanent Court of Arbitration.
See selections listed under *Countries of the World* in Index, Volume 12.

(Continued)

30th—Memorial Day
In 1868, General John A. Logan, Commander-in-Chief of the Grand
Army of the Republic, ordered that May 30th be set aside each
year to decorate the soldiers' graves with flowers . . . "Let no
ravages of time testify to coming generations that we have for-
gotten as a people the cost of a free and undivided Republic."
B.H., 5:137

—— —American Indian Day
This day is observed the second Saturday in May in many states.
See selections listed under *Indians* in Index, Volume 12.

—— —Arbor Day and Bird Day
Arbor Day and Bird Day are celebrated together on the 5th of May
in many states, although the dates of its observance vary widely
according to climate and good planting time, ranging from Decem-
ber to February in the South, and from April to early May in
the North.
For selections see *Holidays–Arbor Day; Nature–Birds; Nature–Trees*
in Index, Volume 12.

—— —I Am an American Day—Often referred to as Citizenship
Recognition Day. Set aside by joint resolution of Congress for the
third Sunday in May and proclaimed annually by the President
"as a public occasion for the recognition of all our citizens who
have attained their majority or who have been naturalized during
the past year."
B.H., 11:173, 216

—— —Mother's Day
Mother's Day is the second Sunday in May. Miss Anna Jarvis of
Philadelphia originated Mother's Day "as a public expression of
our love and reverence for the mothers of our country," and it
was first observed in that city on May 10th, 1908.
B.H., 1:70, 77   B.H., 6:118
B.H., 3:12, 129   B.H., 9:78, 140

—— —National and International Music Week
Starts the first Sunday in May—one of the first national weeks
originated for cultural purposes. "There is comradeship and com-
mon interest in Europe, and North and South America in music."
See selections listed under *Music* in Index, Volume 12.

—— —Poetry Week
Observed the last week in May from Sunday to Sunday
For poets in My BOOK HOUSE see *Poetry* in Index, Volume 12.

Special Events and Famous People in
My BOOK HOUSE who were born in the month of

2nd—P. T. Barnum started his sensational circus tour of our country, 1835.
B.H., 1:105 *Comment, Note*
B.H., 8:143 *Biog.*, 155

10th—Dragon Boat Festival
Holiday in China
B.H., 1:76, 77   B.H., 4:136, 137   B.H., 3:19

11th—The Continental Congress was appointed to draft a declaration of independence.
B.H., 5:120, 121 *Comments*

11th—Kamehameha Day
Hawaiian Festival
B.H., 6:198

14th—Flag Day
Congress formally adopted the stars and stripes as the flag of the
United States on June 14th, 1777. The first public observance of
Flag Day was June 14th, 1897. Almost every home proudly dis-
plays an American Flag on this day.
B.H., 3:46 *Note*   B.H., 11:216   B.H., 5:116

15th—Magna Charta Signed by King John at Runnymede, 1215
B.H., 1:46 *Note*   B.H., 12:218 *Comment*

23rd—William Penn signed the famous treaty of peace and
friendship with the Indians, 1683.
B.H., 9:7 *Comment*

24th—Midsummer Eve and Midsummer Day
"On Midsummer Eve, mortals who watch may see the Fairy Folk."
The summer solstice is celebrated throughout Europe on Midsummer
Eve. As the sun reaches its highest point in the sky at this season,
primitive man associated the fire symbol with this festival, and
consequently huge bonfires are kindled in almost every land.
B.H., 6:36

24th—Battle of Bannockburn, 1314
Secured the Independence of Scotland
B.H., 10:21, 29

25th—Battle of Big Horn, Montana, 1876
"Custer's last stand," his defeat by the Sioux Indians
B.H., 9:73 *Comment*

—— —Father's Day
Mrs. John Bruce Dodd of Spokane, Washington is credited with the
origin of Father's Day. Since 1910, the third Sunday in June has
been set aside as a token of love and respect for fathers.
See selections listed under *Holidays–Father's Day* in Index, Volume
12.

—— —First Day of Summer (Summer Solstice)
We have more hours of daylight and less hours of darkness on this
day than on any other day of the year. "Solstice is the time when
the sun is nearest either pole and farthest from the other."
For selections see *Summer* under *Nature–Seasons* in Index, Volume
12.

Special Events and Famous People in
My BOOK HOUSE who were born in the month of

Special Events and Famous People in
My BOOK HOUSE who were born in the month of

AUGUST

ARTISTS AND ILLUSTRATORS

5th—Maude Petersham (1889-   )
American Artist
Selections in My BOOK HOUSE illustrated
    by Maude and Miska Petersham:
B.H., 3:48, 136   B.H., 8:92, 109
B.H., 4:83   B.H., 10:151, 175, 228
B.H., 6:25, 34   B.H., 12:190
B.H., 7:40, 84

15th—Walter Crane (1845-1915)
English Illustrator, Decorator and Writer
Notes: B.H., 3:26 162, 163

15th—Ivan Meštrović (1883-   )
Yugoslav Sculptor of International Reputa-
    tion; a Leader in the Modern School
B.H., 3:194 (*Illustration*—Horsemen on Lake
    Front)
B.H., 11:29 *Note*

24th—William (Willy) Pogany (1882-   )
Hungarian-American Artist
Selections in My BOOK HOUSE illustrated
    by Willy Pogany:
B.H., 4:104   B.H., 9:140   B.H., 10:217

26th—Franz Hals (1580-1666)
Dutch Portrait Painter
Tales Told in Holland: 152

AUTHORS, PLAYWRIGHTS AND POETS

3rd—Juliana Horatia Ewing (1841-1885)
English Writer for Young People
B.H., 3:29 (*The Owl's Answer to Tommy*)—
    (Story adopted by the Brownie Scouts,
    junior members of the Girl Scout Organ-
    ization)

4th—Percy Bysshe Shelley (1792-1822)
English Poet
B.H., 7:95   B.H., 12:74 *Biog.*
Comments: B.H., 12:54, 72, 93, 96

6th—Alfred Tennyson (1809-1892)
English Poet; Poet Laureate, 1850-1892
For references in My BOOK HOUSE see
    Index, Volume 12

7th—Joseph Rodman Drake (1795-1820)
American Poet
B.H., 6:25

12th—Robert Southey (1774-1843)
English Poet; Poet Laureate, 1813-1843
B.H., 3:20 *Note*
B.H., 7:47
B.H., 12:53 *Comment*, 55

14th—John Galsworthy (1867-1933)
English Novelist and Playwright
B.H., 6:97   B.H., 12:107 *Note*

15th—Sir Walter Scott (1771-1832)
Famous Scottish Poet and Novelist
B.H., 2:217   B.H., 10:20
B.H., 6:70   B.H., 12:108 *Biog.*

24th—Walter Pritchard Eaton (1878-   )
American Author
B.H., 4:79

25th—Francis Bret Harte (1839-1902)
American Poet and Novelist—Writer of
    Western Life
B.H., 12:137 *Comment*

**28th—Johann Wolfgang von Goethe
(1749-1832)**
Outstanding German Poet, Novelist and
    Playwright
B.H., 12:163 *Biog.*, 168, 184 *note*

28th—Leo N. Tolstoy (1828-1910)
Russian Novelist and Social Reformer
B.H., 2:46 B.H., 6:146 B.H., 12:190 *Biog.*

29th—Oliver Wendell Holmes (1809-1894)
New England Poet, Essayist and Physician
B.H., 12:135 *Comment*

29th—Joseph Jacobs (1854-1916)
British Author and Journalist
(Born in Australia)
B.H., 4:134 B.H., 5:156 *Note* B.H., 6:174

MUSICIANS

5th—Ambroise Thomas (1811-1896)
French Composer
B.H., 8:188 *Note*

15th—Samuel Coleridge-Taylor (1875-1912)
British Composer (of African Negro descent)
B.H., 9:89

22nd—Claude Achille Debussy (1862-1918)
French Composer
B.H., 3:151 *Note* B.H., 6:144

OTHER FAMOUS PEOPLE

9th—Henry V (1387-1422)
King of England
B.H., 1:41 *Note* B.H., 12:219 *Comment*

15th—Napoleon I (1769-1821)
Emperor of the French (Corsican by birth)
B.H., 8:163 *Comment*

19th—Orville Wright (1871-   )
Aviator and Inventor
B.H., 5:66

26th—Albert (Francis Charles Augustus Albert Emmanuel) (1819-1861)
Prince Consort of England—Husband of Queen Victoria
B.H., 8:158 *Comments*

SPECIAL EVENTS IN AUGUST

2nd—United States War Department purchased first plane from Wright brothers in 1909, thus founding the Army Air Corps.
B.H., 5:66

5th—Civil War Battle of Mobile Bay, 1864, with Admiral Farragut in command
B.H., 8:82

11th—The Clermont, Fulton's First Steamboat, made a successful trip from New York to Albany, 1807.
B.H., 1:97 (Picture of a Steamboat)
B.H., 5:48
For other selections see *Transportation–Boats* in Index, Volume 12.

15th—Panama Canal Opened to the commerce of the world, 1914
B.H., 9:77 *Comment*

21st—Lincoln-Douglas Debates Began, 1858
B.H., 5:134 *Comment, Picture*

Special Events and Famous People in
My BOOK HOUSE who were born in the month of

SEPTEMBER

212

13th—Eugen Krantz (1844-1898)
German Composer
B.H., 2:70 Note

26th—George Gershwin (1898-1937)
American Composer
B.H., 3:185 Note

7th—Elizabeth, Queen of England (1533-1603)
Comments: B.H., 12:15, 26, 30, 31, 220 Picture
Notes: B.H., 1:44, 49, 50
B.H., 12:29, 31, 107

8th—Richard I (Richard the Lionhearted) (1157-1199)
King of England
B.H., 6:160 Comment   B.H., 10:32 Note

OTHER FAMOUS PEOPLE

6th—Marquis de Lafayette (1757-1834)
French General, Patriot and Friend of America
During the Revolutionary War
B.H., 5:125 Picture, Note

SPECIAL EVENTS IN SEPTEMBER

12th—Hudson River Entered 1609 by Henry Hudson, an English navigator in the service of Holland. This is the river on which Robert Fulton's steamboat, the Clermont, made its first trip.
B.H., 5:52 Comment

17th—Constitution Day
The Constitution of the United States was adopted in 1787. It was framed by the Constitutional Convention that met in Philadelphia. The Constitution of the United States ranks above every other written constitution for the simplicity, brevity and precision of its language.

—— —Autumnal Equinox—First Day of Autumn
The date varies from September 21st to 23rd. See Vernal Equinox in March Calendar for definition.
For selections in My BOOK HOUSE see Seasons–Autumn under Nature in Index, Volume 12.

—— —Labor Day
Celebrated each year on the first Monday in September. This holiday was first celebrated in 1882 by the Knights of Labor in New York. Many parades, picnics, games and meetings are held on this day by labor leaders and workers. The Labor Day parade is really a survival of the medieval processions of the guilds. Richard Wagner presents one of these processions in his opera, Die Meistersinger von Nürnberg.
For selections in My BOOK HOUSE see Occupations in Index, Volume 12.

Special Events and Famous People in
My BOOK HOUSE who were born in the month of

OCTOBER

22nd—Franz Liszt (1811-1886)
Hungarian Composer and Conductor
B.H., 7:11 *Note*   B.H., 11:163 *Note*

25th—Johann Strauss (1825-1899)
Austrian Composer
"The Beautiful Blue Danube" is the most
celebrated of more than five hundred waltzes
composed by Johann Strauss.
B.H., 9:172 *Note*

28th—Howard Hanson (1896-   )
American Composer and Orchestral Conductor
B.H., 10:81 *Note*

OTHER FAMOUS PEOPLE

14th—William Penn (1644-1718)
English Quaker, Founder of the Colony of
   Pennsylvania
B.H., 9:7 *Comment*

21st—Alfred Bernhard Nobel (1833-1896)
Swedish Chemist and Manufacturer; inventor
   of dynamite, patron of peace—founder of
   the Nobel Prizes
Nobel Prize Winners in My BOOK HOUSE:
   Björnstjerne Björnson; Anatole France;
   John Galsworthy; Rudyard Kipling; Theo-
   dore Roosevelt; Rabindranath Tagore;
   Woodrow T. Wilson

27th—Theodore Roosevelt (1858-1919)
Twenty-Sixth President of the United States
B.H., 9:66, 72 *Biog.*

28th—Captain James Cook (1728-1779)
English Naval Captain and Explorer
B.H., 8:149, 150 *Comments*

SPECIAL EVENTS IN OCTOBER

12th—Columbus Day
America's Anniversary in Honor of Christopher Columbus and His
   Discovery of America, 1492
B.H., 5:112

25th—Battle of Agincourt, 1415
One of the Great Battles of the Hundred Years War between
   France and England
B.H., 12:219 *Comment*

27th—Navy Day
Observed since 1922 to commemorate the birthday of the United
   States Navy in 1775
See selections listed under *Transportation–Boats* in Index, Volume 12.

28th—Statue of Liberty Dedicated, 1886
The French people raised money and sent us our own Statue of
   Liberty as a gift to celebrate our hundredth anniversary of inde-
   pendence in America. A famous artist, M. Frédéric Bartholdi,
   designed it.
B.H., 11:172, 173

31st—Hallowe'en
See selections listed under *Holidays–Hallowe'en* in Index, Volume 12.
See also Unit No. 6, pages 9-10, of *Creative Work for Your Child's
   Hands.*

Special Events and Famous People in
My BOOK HOUSE who were born in the month of

NOVEMBER

25th—Ethelbert Nevin (1862-1901)
American Composer
B.H., 9:140 *Note*   B.H., 10:11 *Note*

28th—Anton Rubinstein (1829-1894)
Russian Pianist and Composer
B.H., 2:81 *Note*

OTHER FAMOUS PEOPLE

2nd—Marie Antoinette (1755-1793)
Nursery Friends from France: 76 *Picture, Note*

2nd—Daniel Boone (1734-1820)
One of the Greatest Wilderness Hunters and
    Scouts
B.H., 9:7, 67 *Comment*

14th—Robert Fulton (1765-1815)
American Engineer, Miniature Painter and
    Inventor of the Steamboat
B.H., 5:48

19th—Charles I (1600-1649)
King of Great Britain and Ireland
B.H., 1:45 *Note*   B.H., 12:29 *Note*

19th—George Rogers Clark (1752-1818)
Soldier and Surveyor—Leader of the Con-
    quest of the Northwest
B.H., 9:66

20th—Amos Bronson Alcott (1799-1888)
American Visionary Philosopher and Social
    Dreamer; "great pioneer in the field of
    American education"
Father of Louisa M. Alcott
B.H., 12:122

SPECIAL EVENTS IN NOVEMBER

1st-7th—American Art Week
For artists in My BOOK HOUSE see *Artists and Illustrators* in
    Index, Volume 12.

**19th—Abraham Lincoln Delivered His Famous "Gettysburg
Address"** in 1863 to honor the Northern soldiers who had fallen
    during the Battle of Gettysburg—July 1st to 3rd, 1863.
B.H., 5:137

21st—Mayflower Compact Signed 1620
"On the very day the Mayflower anchored in what is now Cape
    Cod Harbor, the Pilgrim Fathers signed the famous paper known
    as the 'Mayflower Compact' which provided a form of govern-
    ment 'in which they agreed to be governed by such rules and reg-
    ulations as should be made by common consent for the good of all'."
B.H., 5:113

——— —American Education Week
Observed during the week in which Armistice Day falls

——— —Children's Book Week
Announced annually—usually dated about the middle of November

——— —Thanksgiving Day
B.H., 1:87, 216   B.H., 6:79
B.H., 4:80   B.H., 7:72
B.H., 5: 113, 115

Special Events and Famous People in
My BOOK HOUSE who were born in the month of

DECEMBER

ARTISTS

3rd—Gilbert Stuart (1755-1828)
American Portrait Painter
B.H., 5:124 *Note*

AUTHORS AND POETS

1st—Oliver Herford (1863-1935)
American Author, Illustrator
B.H., 3:39

5th—Christina Rossetti (1830-1894)
English Poetess
B.H., 1:156, 157, 201 B.H., 12:145 *Comment*
B.H., 2:105

6th—Joseph Conrad (1857-1924)
English Novelist, Born in Poland
B.H., 12:107 *Note*

8th—Björnstjerne Bjornson (1832-1910)
Norwegian Poet, Dramatist and Novelist
B.H., 3:137   B.H., 12:187 *Biog.*

9th—Joel Chandler Harris (1848-1908)
Southern Writer—famous for his Negro folk
  tales and his "Uncle Remus" stories
B.H., 3:123
B.H., 12:137 *Comment*, 138 *Biog.*

9th—John Milton (1608-1674)
England's Great Puritan Poet and Author of
  "Paradise Lost"
B.H., 7:122 *Note*, 159
B.H., 12:29 *Note*

10th—George MacDonald (1824-1905)
Scotch Poet and Novelist, Minister
B.H., 5:186

10th—Emily Dickinson (1830-1886)
New England Poetess
B.H., 3:155   B.H., 12:153 *Note*

13th—Heinrich Heine (1797-1856)
German Lyric Poet
B.H., 2:138

16th—Jane Austen (1775-1817)
English Novelist
B.H., 12:101 *Note*

17th—John Greenleaf Whittier
(1807-1892)
New England Poet and Writer
B.H., 4:23
B.H., 12:118 *Biog.*, 137 *Comment*

21st—Jean Henri Fabre (1823-1915)
French Naturalist and Writer
B.H., 6:184 *Biog.*

24th—William Brighty Rands (1823-1882)
English Juvenile and Miscellaneous Writer
  Known as "The Laureate of the Nursery"
B.H., 3:11   B.H., 4:11

30th—Rudyard Kipling (1865-1936)
English Poet and Story Writer
B.H., 9:129   B.H., 12:107 *Note*

31st—Pamela Bianco (1906-   )
English Illustrator and Author
B.H., 3:91

MUSICIANS

7th—Rudolph Friml (1884-   )
Bohemian Composer and Pianist
B.H., 9:120 *Note*

218

8th—Jean Sibelius (1865-   )
Finnish Composer
B.H., 10:154 *Note*

11th—Hector Berlioz (1803-1869)
French Composer
B.H., 2:185
B.H., 4:147 *Note*
B.H., 12:171 *Note*

16th—Ludwig van Beethoven (1770-1827)
German Composer
Notes: B.H., 2:40
       B.H., 3:42
       B.H., 12:185

18th—Edward Alexander MacDowell (1861-1908)
American Composer and Pianist
B.H., 3:134
Notes: B.H., 3:126
       B.H., 5:209
       B.H., 10:11
       B.H., 11:58

18th—Carl Maria von Weber (1786-1826)
German Composer
B.H., 3:110 *Note*

22nd—Deems Taylor (1885-   )
American Composer
B.H., 3:171 *Note*

24th—Charles Wakefield Cadman (1881-   )
American Composer
B.H., 3:61 *Note*

OTHER FAMOUS PEOPLE

5th—George Armstrong Custer (1839-1876)
American Cavalry Officer and Indian Fighter
B.H., 9:73 *Comment*

24th—Christopher (Kit) Carson (1809-1868)
Hunter, Trapper, Guide and Western Scout
B.H., 9:35 *Comment*

28th—Woodrow Wilson (1856-1924)
Twenty-Eighth President of the United States
B.H., 11:216

31st—Charles Edward Stuart (Bonnie Prince Charlie) (1720-1788)
English Prince (Called the Young Pretender)
Notes: B.H., 1:34, 99, 115

SPECIAL EVENTS IN DECEMBER

17th—First Successful Airplane Flight Made by Wright Brothers at Kitty Hawk, N.C., 1903.
B.H., 5:66

25th—Washington Crossed the Delaware to Attack Trenton, 1776.
B.H. 5:124 *Comment*

25th—Christmas Day
See selections listed under *Holidays–Christmas* in Index, Volume 12.
See also Unit No. 6, pages 11-12 of *Creative Work for Your Child's Hands.*

——Beginning of the Winter Season (Winter Solstice)
This is the shortest day of the year. See Summer Solstice in June Calendar for definition.
For selections see *Seasons–Winter* under *Nature* in Index, Volume 12.